Drag and Drop
Windows 7

Davinder Singh Minhas

STERLING

STERLING PUBLISHERS PVT. LTD.
A-59, Okhla Industrial Area, Phase-II, New Delhi
Ph.: 26386165, 26387070, 26386209
Fax: 91-11-26383788
E-mail: mail@sterlingpublishers.com
Website: www.sterlingpublishers.com

ISBN: 978-81-207-5743-1

© 2011, Windows 7

All rights reserved. No part of this publication may be reproduced, stored in a retrieval system, or transmitted, in any form or by any means, electronic, mechanical, photocopying, recording or otherwise, without the prior permission of the original publishers.

Printed at Sterling Publishers Private Limited., New Delhi-110020. India

Contents

Introduction 5

Personalizing windows 13

Windows accessories 21

Files and folders 24

Playing a music CD 37

Optimizing performance 39

1 Introduction

Windows 7

Windows 7 is the latest operating system from Microsoft. It is a program that controls the overall activity of your computer. Microsoft Windows 7 ensures that all parts of your computer work together, smoothly and efficiently.

There are many ways in which you can manage the files stored on your computer. You can open, rename, print, delete, move and search for files. You can also e-mail a file.

Windows 7 provides many ways to work with images. You can create your own picture. You can import images from a scanner, a digital camera or download images from the Internet.

Windows 7 allows you to play music CDs, watch DVD Movies and it also helps you find the latest music and movies on the Internet.

You can connect your computer to the Internet and browse the World Wide Web. You can search for Web pages of your interest. You can also exchange electronic mail with people in Windows Vista.

Windows 7 is available in six different editions, but only **Home Premium**, **Professional** and **Ultimate** are widely available. The other editions are focused at other markets, such as the developing world, or for enterprise use.

Drag and Drop Series

WINDOWS 7 SCREEN

Before working in Windows 7, you must understand the basic screen elements.

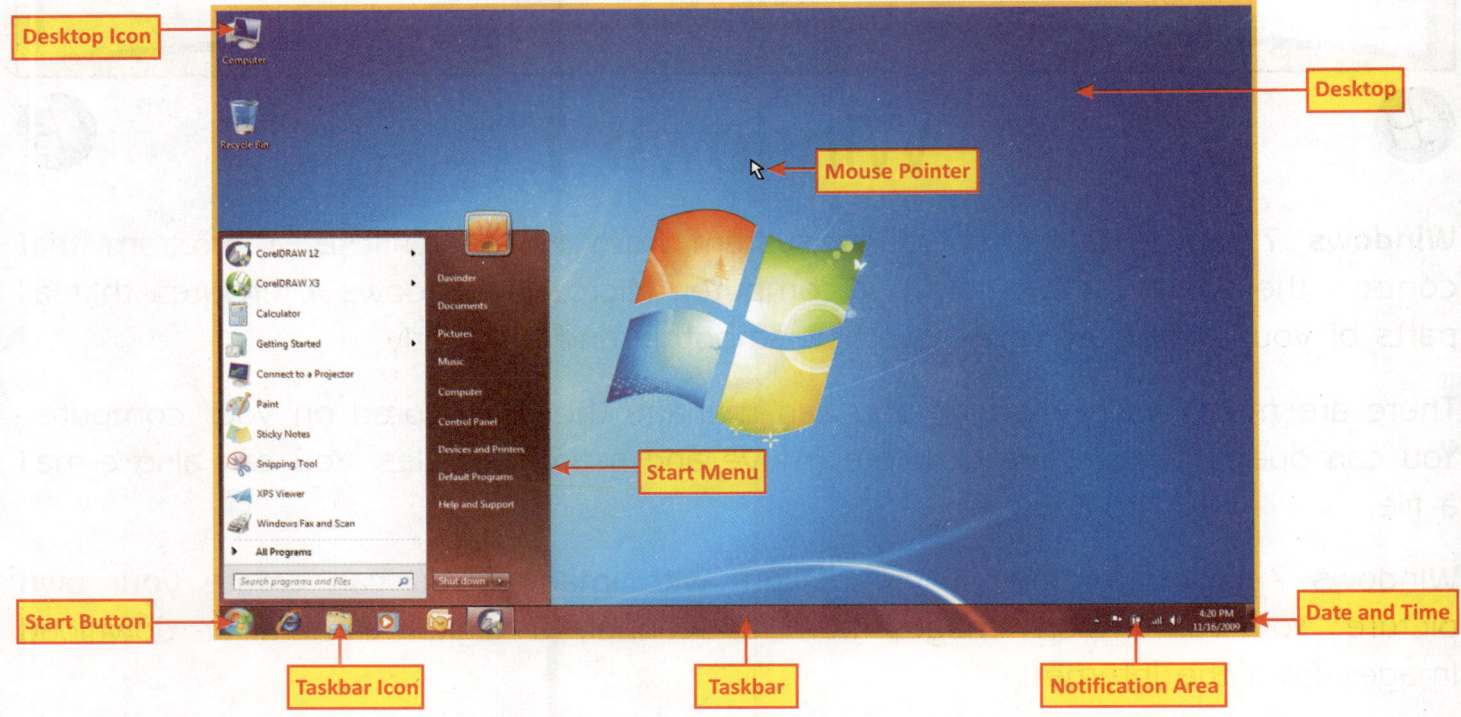

Desktop Icon: An icon on the desktop represents a program or Windows 7 feature. A program you install often adds its own icon on the desktop.

Mouse Pointer: When you move your mouse, this pointer moves along with it.

Desktop: This is the Windows 7 'work area,' meaning that it is where you work with your programs and documents.

Time and Date: This is the current time and date on your computer. To see the full date, position the mouse on the time. To change the date or time, click on it.

Notification Area: This area displays small icons that notify you about things that are happening on your computer. For example, you see notifications if your printer runs out of paper or if an update to Windows 7 is available over the Internet.

Taskbar: The programs you have opened appear in the taskbar. You use this area to switch between programs if you have more than one running at a time.

Taskbar Icons: You use these icons to launch some Windows 7 features with just a mouse click.

Start Button: You use this button to start the programs and launch many features of the Windows 7.

Start Menu: Start menu lists all the installed programs in the computer.

START A PROGRAM

You can open a program in Windows 7 by using the Start menu. Windows 7 opens the program and displays it on the desktop.

1. Click on the **Start** button.

2. Click on **All Programs** to view a list of the programs present on the hard disk.

A list of the programs appears.

All Programs button changes to **Back** button.

3. Click on the program you want to open.

Some programs have a sub-menu.

In this example we choose **Accessories**.

Accessories sub-menu will appear.

Drag and Drop Series

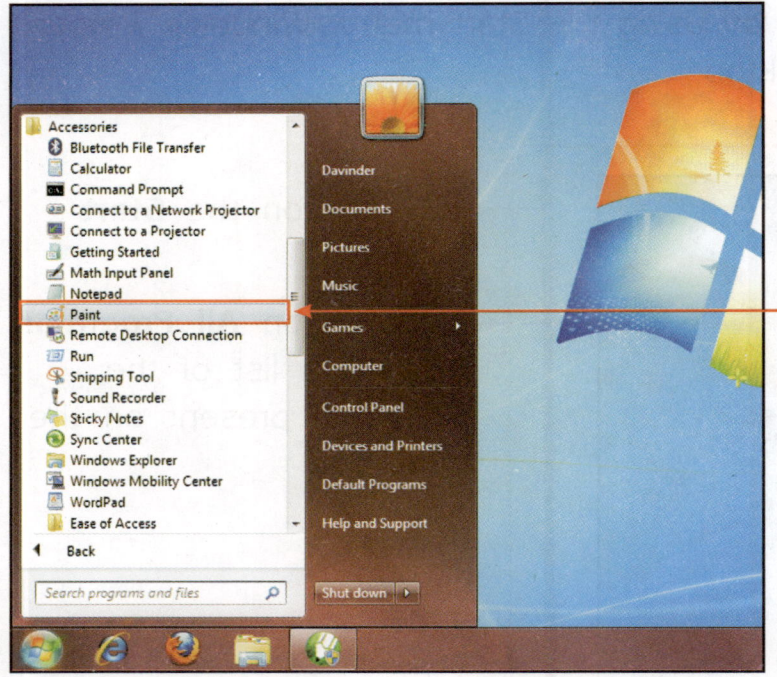

4. Click on **Paint** from the Accessories sub-menu.

The Paint window will appear.

Windows 7 adds an icon for the program to the **taskbar**.

8

MAXIMIZE WINDOW

With the help of the maximize button, you can enlarge a window to its maximum size.

To maximize the window:

1. Click on the **Maximize** button in the window.

The window fills your screen.

2. Click on the **Restore Down** button to return the window to its previous size.

MINIMIZE WINDOW

You can minimize the window to remove it from your screen, if you are not using that window. You can re-display the window any time by clicking on its icon in the taskbar.

To minimize the window:

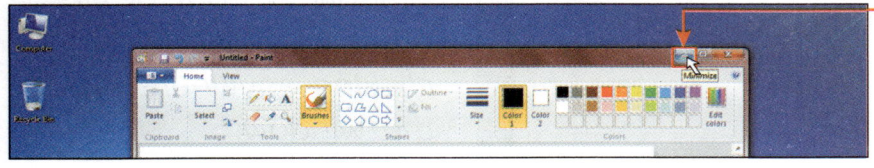

1. Click on the **Minimize** button in the window.

The window reduces to an icon in the taskbar.

2. To re-display the window, click on the icon of the window in the taskbar.

Drag and Drop Series

SWITCH BETWEEN WINDOW

If you have more than one window open on your screen, you can easily switch between the windows. You can switch from one program to another using either the taskbar or the switch between windows button.

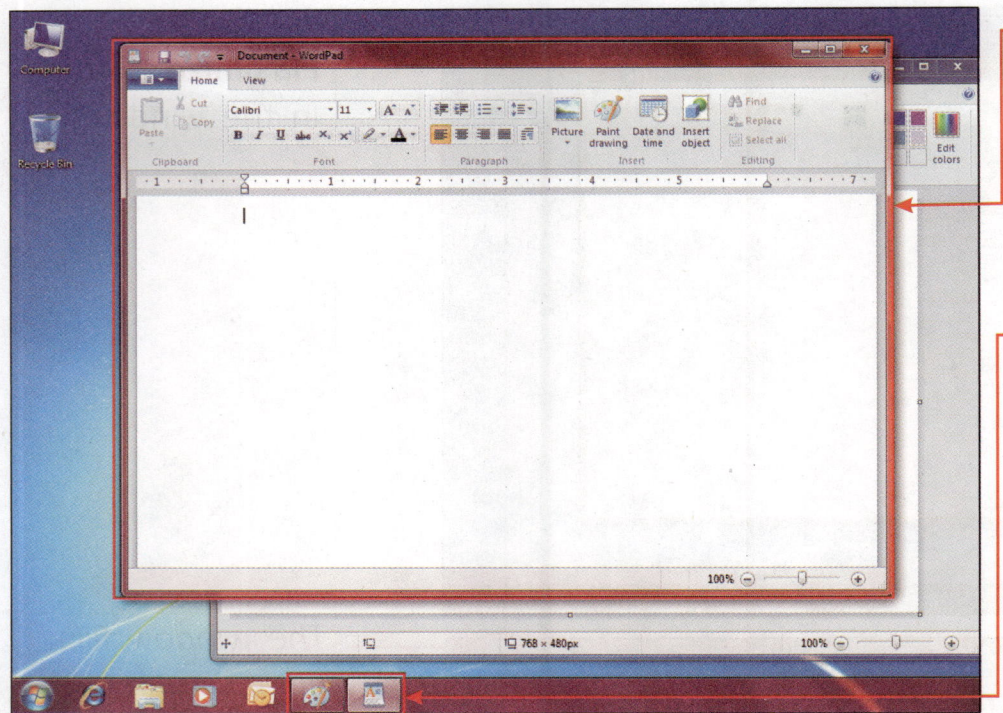

You can work only in one window at a time. The active window appears in front of all other windows and displays a dark title bar.

The **taskbar** displays an icon for each open window on your screen.

1. To display the window you want to work with click on its icon on the taskbar.

The window appears in the forefront. You can now clearly view the contents of the window.

You can also display a window in front of all other windows by clicking anywhere inside the window.

SHOW DESKTOP USING AERO PEEK

In the far right corner of the taskbar there is now the Aero Peek button. You can instantly minimize all your open windows to remove them from your screen to clearly view the desktop.

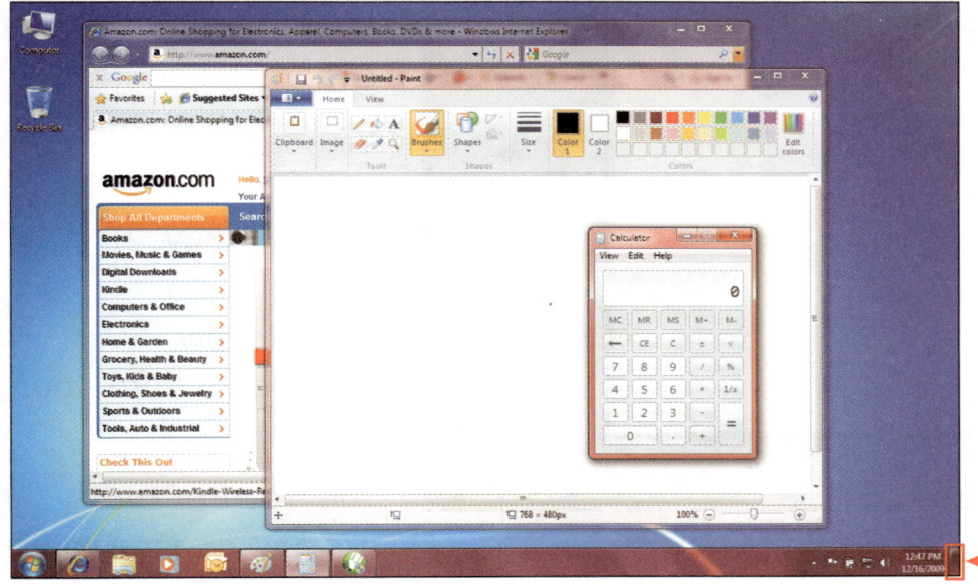

1. Take your mouse pointer on the **Show Desktop** button.

When you hover the mouse pointer on the Show Desktop button, all the windows becomes transparent.

You can see the desktop.

2. Now click on the **Show Desktop** button.

Each window minimizes to an icon in the taskbar. You can now clearly view the desktop.

If you want to redisplay all the windows, click on **Show Desktop** again.

To display only one window, click on its icon in the taskbar.

Drag and Drop Series

CLOSE A WINDOW

You can close the window to remove it from your screen after finishing your work.

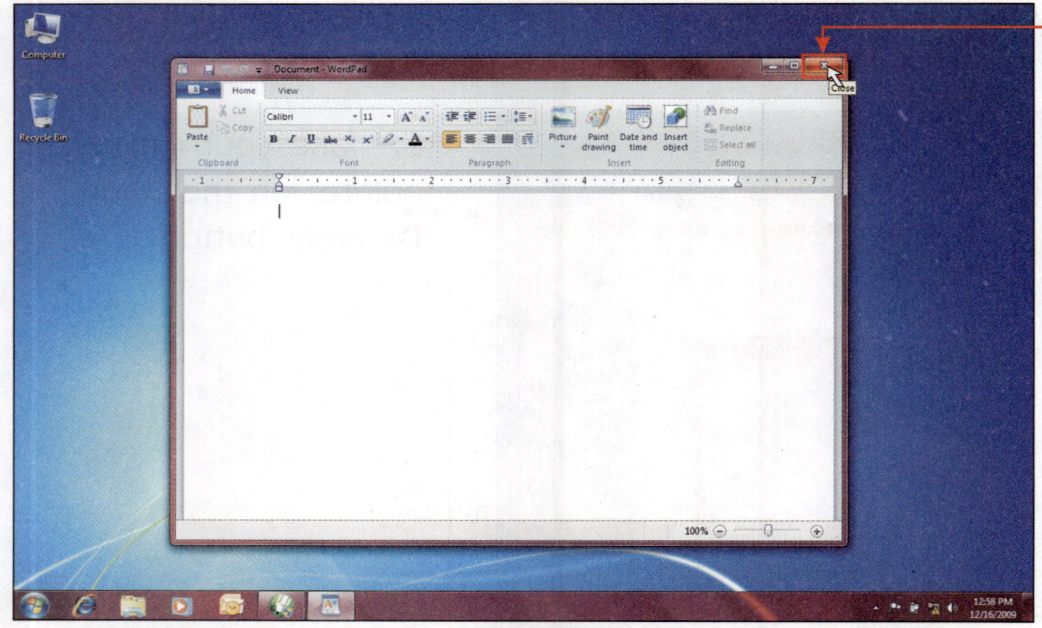

1. Click on the **Close** button in the window.

Or

You can press **Alt + F4** as a shortcut key.

The window disappears from your screen.

The icon of the window disappears from the taskbar.

SHUTTING DOWN WINDOWS 7

Once you have finished your work, you need to shut down your computer.

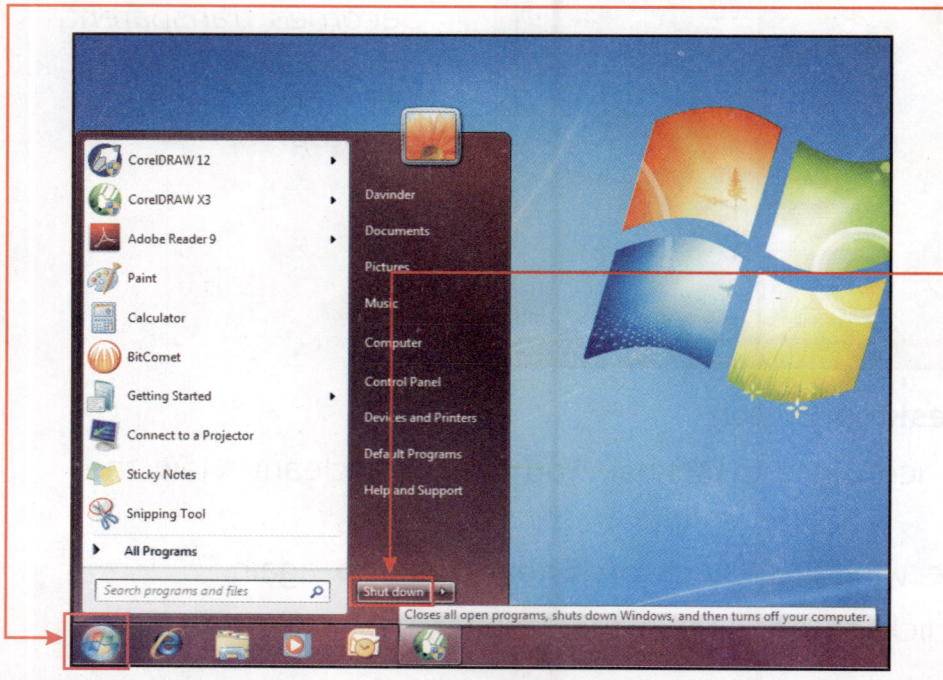

1. Click on the **Start** button.

The start menu will appear.

2. Click on **Shut Down**.

Windows shuts down and turns off the computer.

2. Personalizing windows

CHANGING THE DESKTOP BACKGROUND

You can select a picture, a background color, or both to enhance the appearance of your desktop. You can use your own picture or the picture that Windows provides to add a background to your desktop.

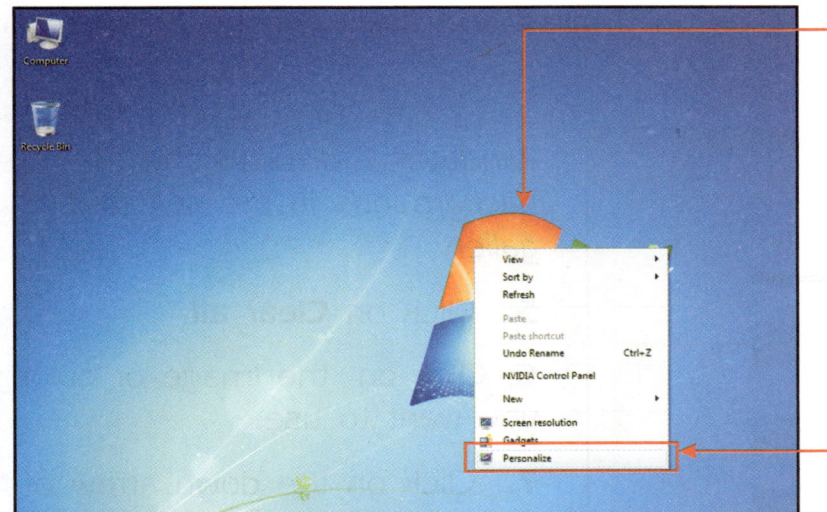

1. Right-click your mouse on a blank area in your desktop.

   A menu will appear.

2. Click on **Personalize** in the menu.

   *The **Personalization** window appears.*

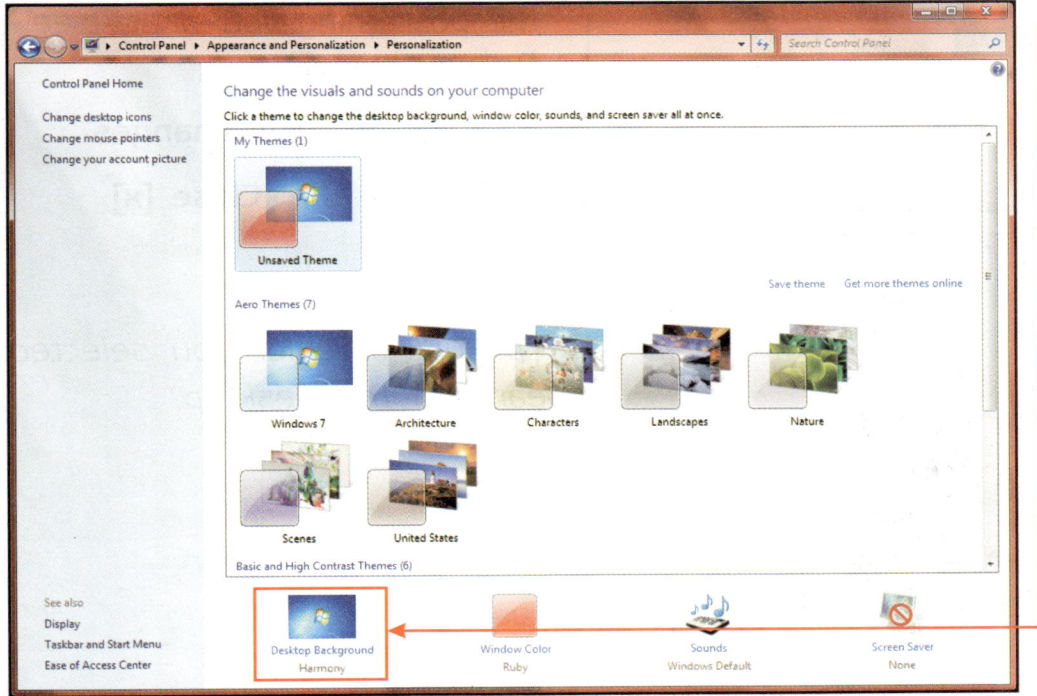

3. Click on **Desktop Background**.

   The Desktop Background window appears.

Drag and Drop Series

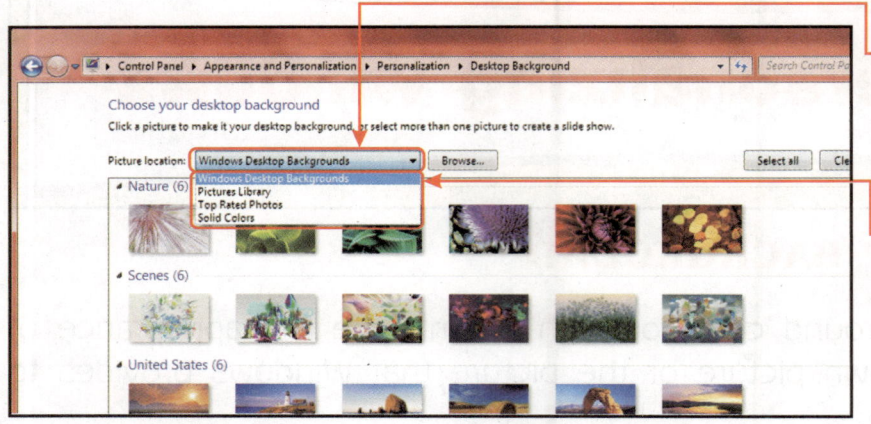

4. Click on the down arrow of **Picture location**.

A menu will appear.

5. Click on the background gallery you want to use.

You can click on **Pictures Library** in the list if you want to add your own image as the desktop background. You can also click on **Browse** and then use the Browse dialog box to select the file.

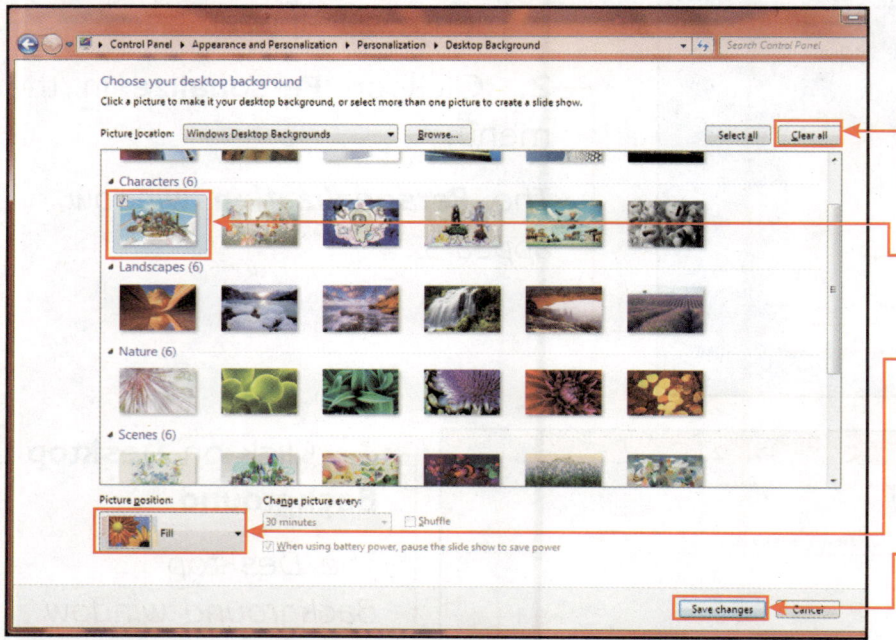

Windows 7 displays the backgrounds in the selected gallery.

5. Click on **Clear all**.

6. Click on the image or color you want to use.

7. Click on the down arrow of **Picture position** and then click the positioning you want. (see **Do you know?**)

8. Click on **Save changes**.

9. Click on the **Close [x]** button.

The picture or color you selected appears on the desktop.

14

Windows 7

SET THE SCREEN SAVER

You can set up Windows 7 to display a screen saver, a moving pattern or a series of pictures. The screen saver is the moving picture that appears automatically on your computer, if you do not use your computer for a period of time.

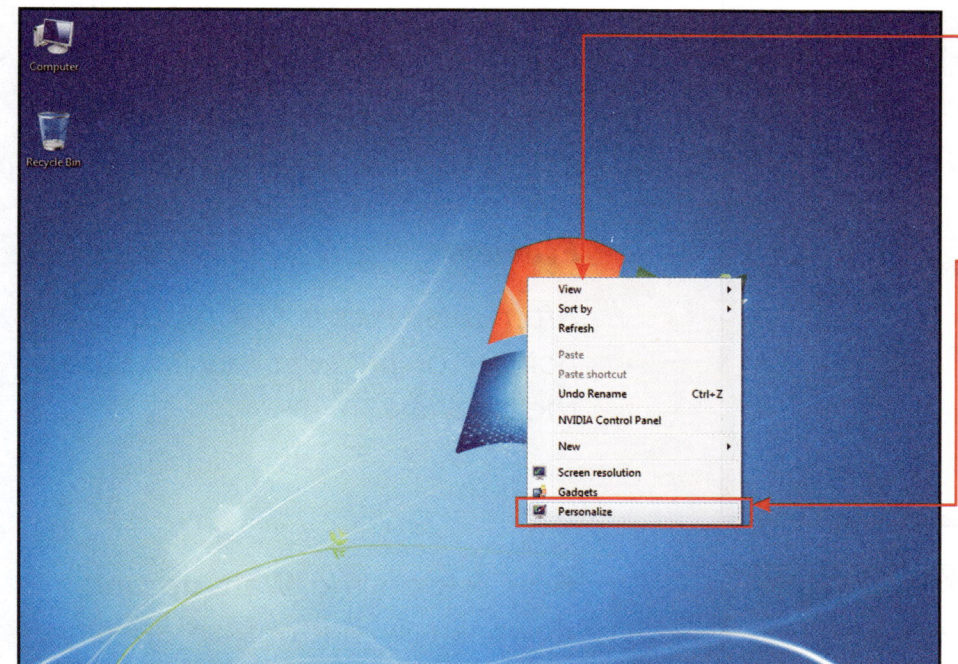

1. Right-click your mouse on a blank area of your desktop.

   A menu will appear.

2. Click on **Personalize** in the menu.

   *The **Personalization** window appears.*

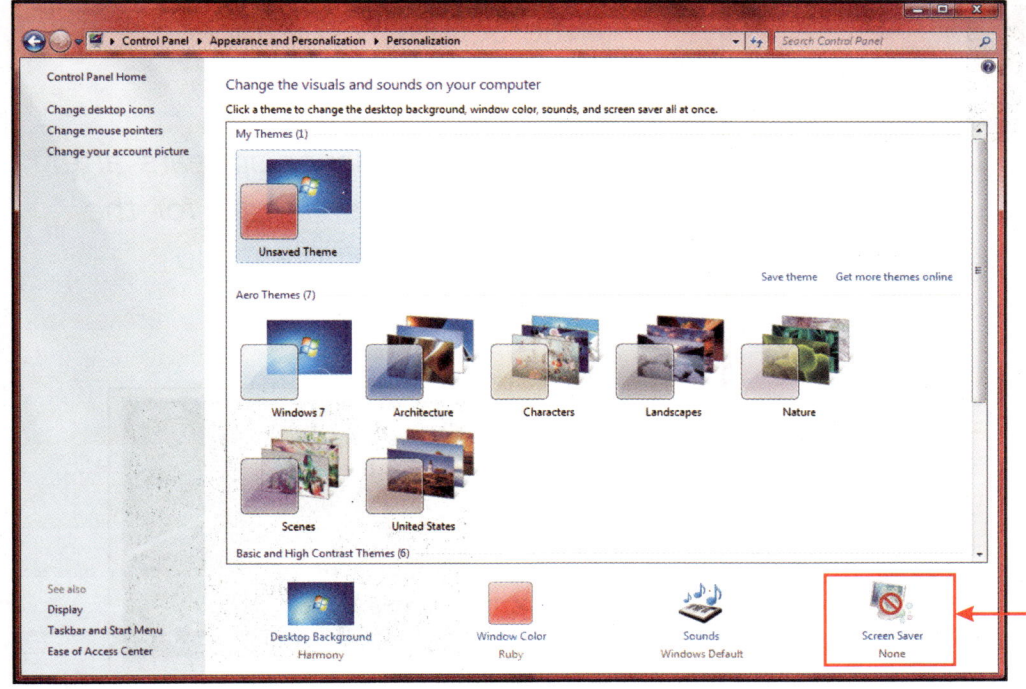

3. Click on **Screen Saver**.

   *The **Screen Saver Setting** dialog box appears.*

15

Drag and Drop Series

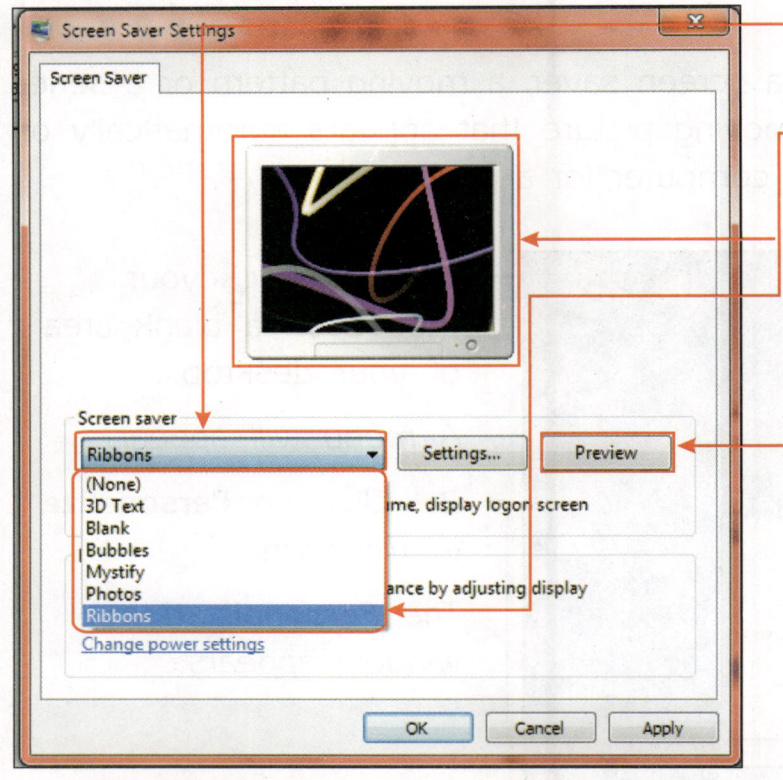

4. Click on the down arrow of **Screen saver**.

5. Click on the screen saver you want to use.

A preview of the screen saver appears.

Note: *All screen savers cannot display the small preview. To see an actual preview, click on* ***Preview****.*

After this, move the mouse pointer or press a key to stop the preview.

6. Click on the **Wait up** and **down** arrow buttons to specify the number of minutes of computer idle time after which the screen saver appears.

7. Click on **OK**.

The screen saver appears after your computer is idle for the number of minutes you specified in Step 6.

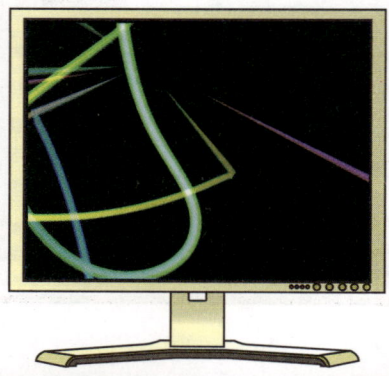

Windows 7

CHANGE THE COLOR SCHEME

You can personalize your Windows 7 by choosing a different color scheme, which it applies to the window borders, taskbar, and Start menu. The Aero color scheme is a new color scheme in Windows 7 which shows new transparencies, live thumbnails, live icons, animations and eye candy.

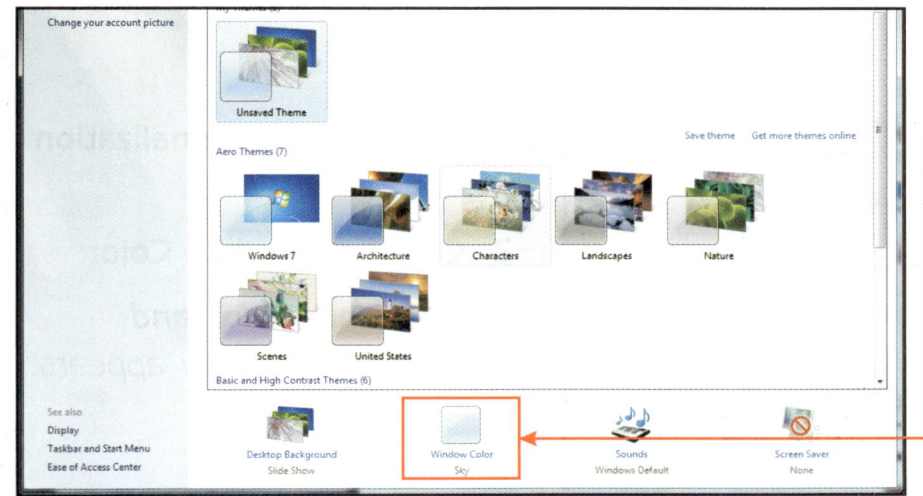

1. Open the **Personalization** window.

2. Click on **Window Color**.

   The **Window Color and Appearance** window appears.

3. Click on the **color** you want to use.

   Windows immediately changes the color of the window border.

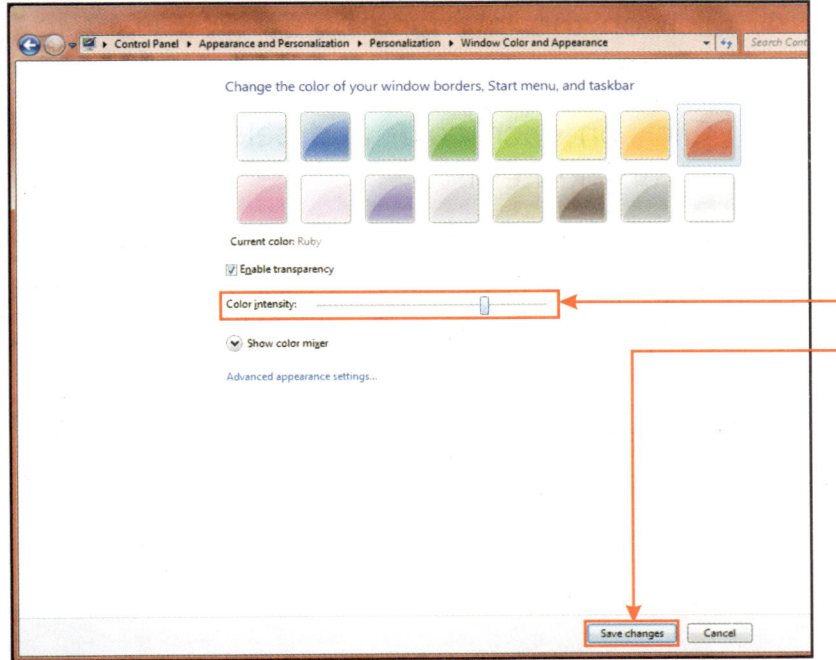

4. To set the color intensity, click and drag the **Color intensity** slider.

   Windows changes the transparency and intensity of the window border.

5. Click on **Save changes**.

   Windows applies the new color scheme.

Drag and Drop Series

If your computer has a **lower-end graphics card** or little **graphics memory**, Windows 7 is unable to use the effects (shown in this section) such as **transparency** and **color intensity**.

In that case you will see the Window Color and Appearance dialog box instead of the window.

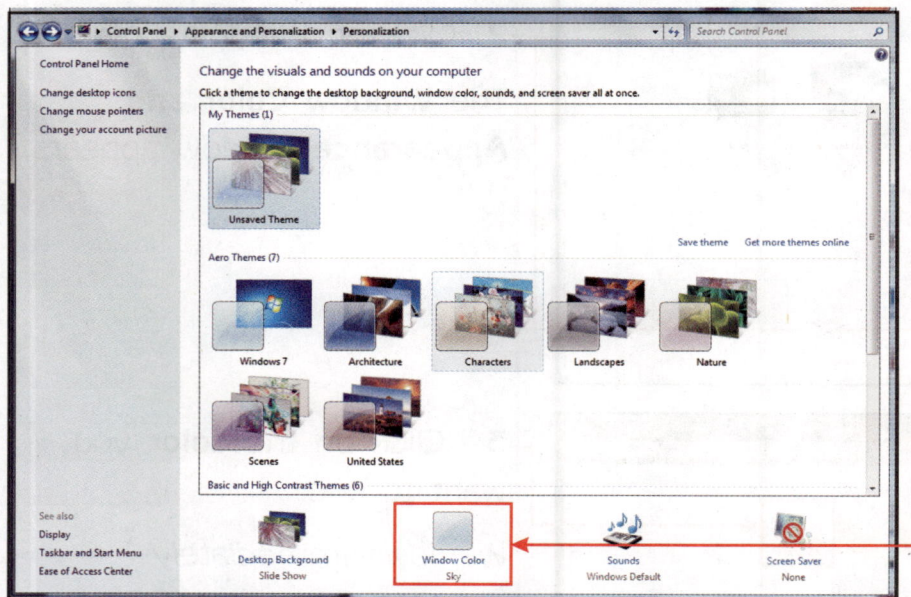

1. Open the **Personalization** window.

2. Click on **Window Color**.

   *The **Window Color and Appearance** window appears.*

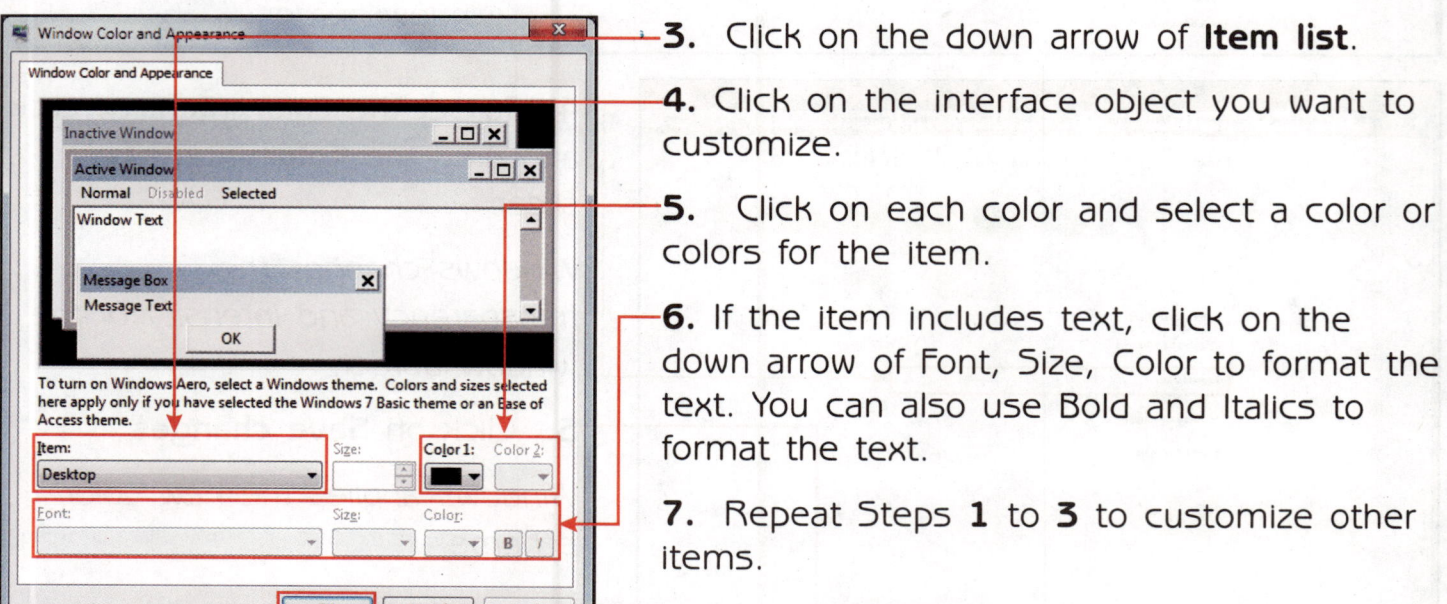

3. Click on the down arrow of **Item list**.

4. Click on the interface object you want to customize.

5. Click on each color and select a color or colors for the item.

6. If the item includes text, click on the down arrow of Font, Size, Color to format the text. You can also use Bold and Italics to format the text.

7. Repeat Steps **1** to **3** to customize other items.

8. Click on **OK**.

Windows 7

ADD A GADGET TO THE SIDEBAR

You can make the Windows desktop more useful by adding gadgets to it. A gadget is a small program such as a clock or calculator that performs a specific function.

Add a gadget

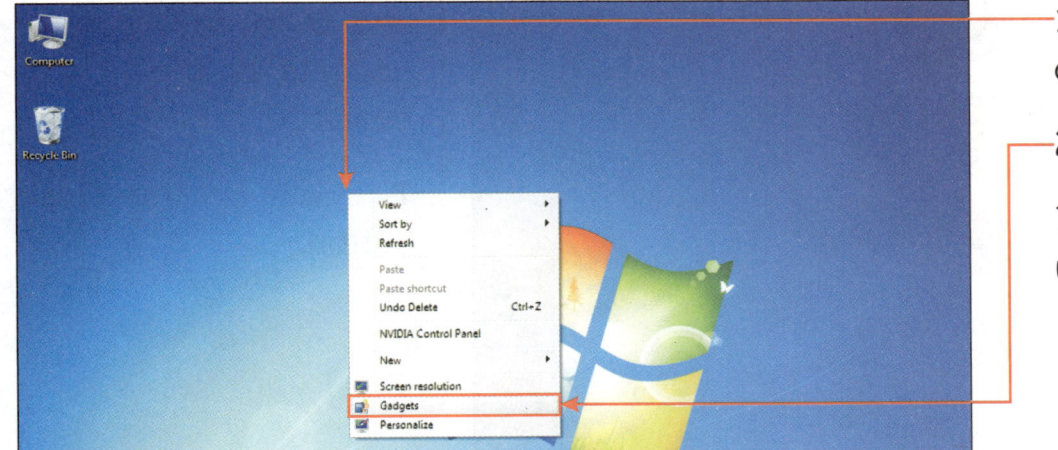

1. **Right-click** on the desktop.

2. Click on **Gadgets**.

   *The **Gadget Gallery** will appear.*

3. Click on a **gadget**.

   *You can click on **Show details** to see the description of the gadget.*

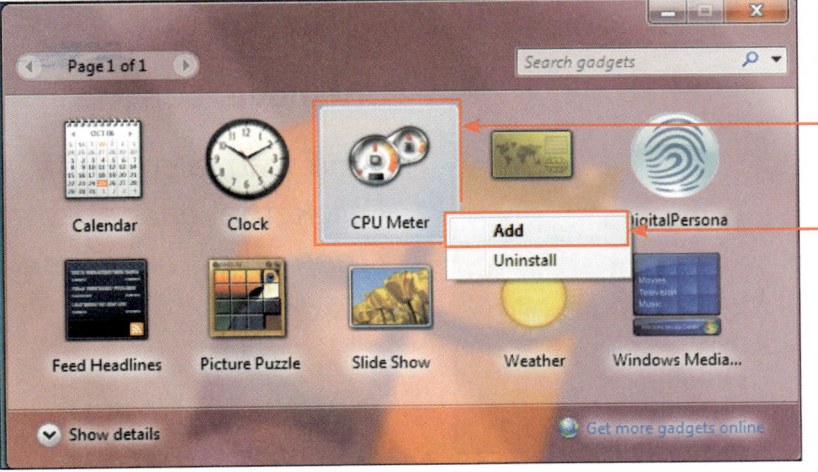

4. Right-click the gadget, If you want to add it.

5. Click on **Add**.

   You can also double-click the gadget.

19

Windows 7 adds the gadget to the desktop.

6. Repeat Steps **4** and **5** to add more gadgets to the desktop.

7. Click on the **Close** button.

Remove a gadget

You can remove the gadget from the desktop when you do not use it.

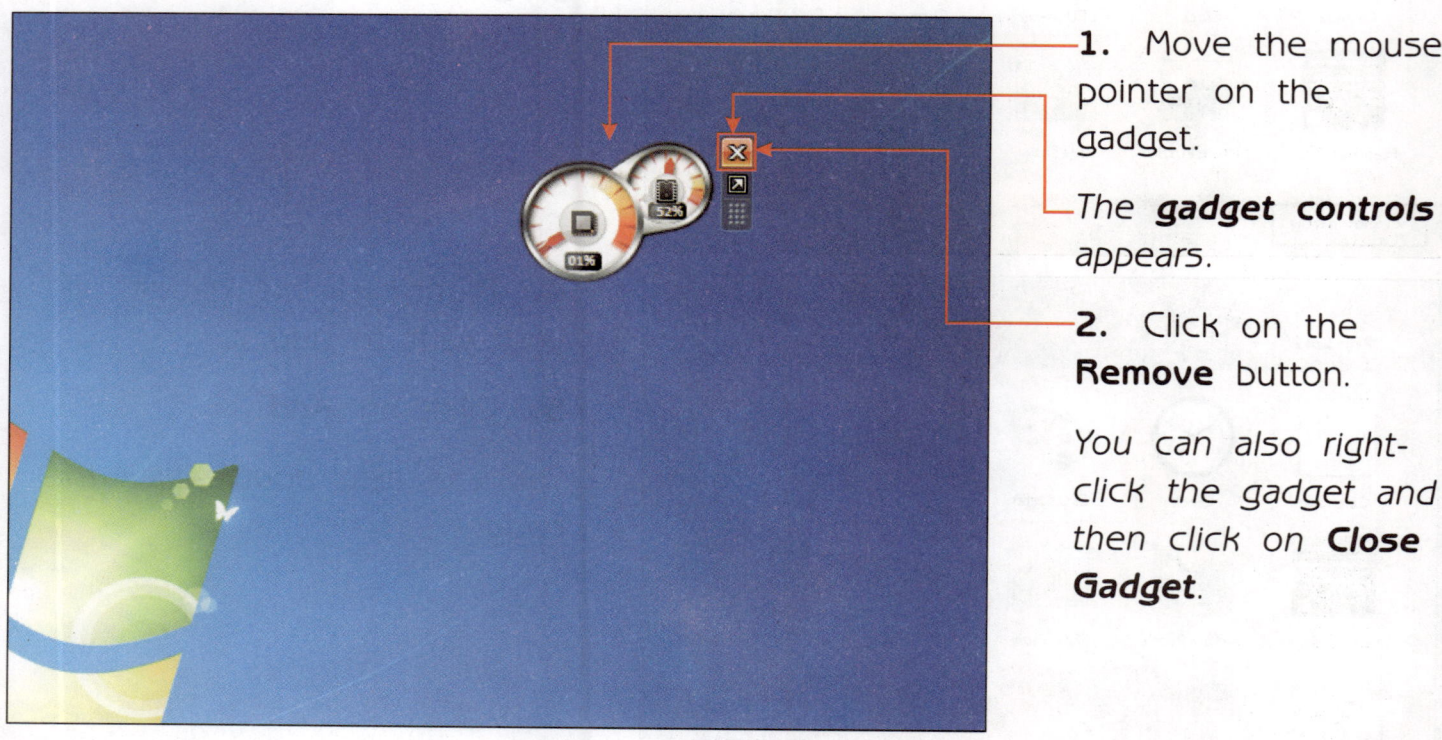

1. Move the mouse pointer on the gadget.

*The **gadget controls** appears.*

2. Click on the **Remove** button.

*You can also right-click the gadget and then click on **Close Gadget**.*

3   Windows accessories

WORKING WITH WORDPAD

What made the personal computer attractive was that one could type a document on it, save it, and then edit it later to correct grammatical errors and typing mistakes without having to re-type the entire document. One cannot do these things on a typewriter.

Windows comes with a basic word processing program called **WordPad** that you can use to type, format, and print documents, such as letters and reports.

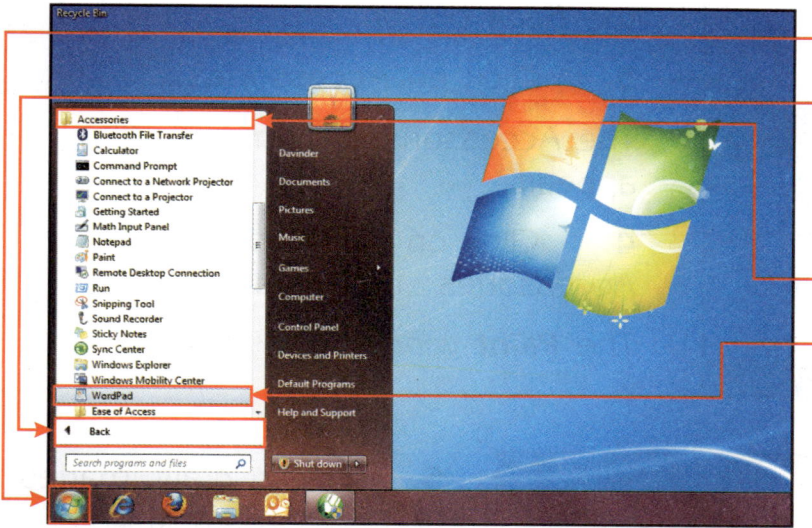

1. Click on the **Start** button.

2. Click on **All Programs.**

   The **All Programs** button changes to the **Back** button.

3. Click on **Accessories.**

4. Click on **WordPad**.

   WordPad starts and displays a blank document window.

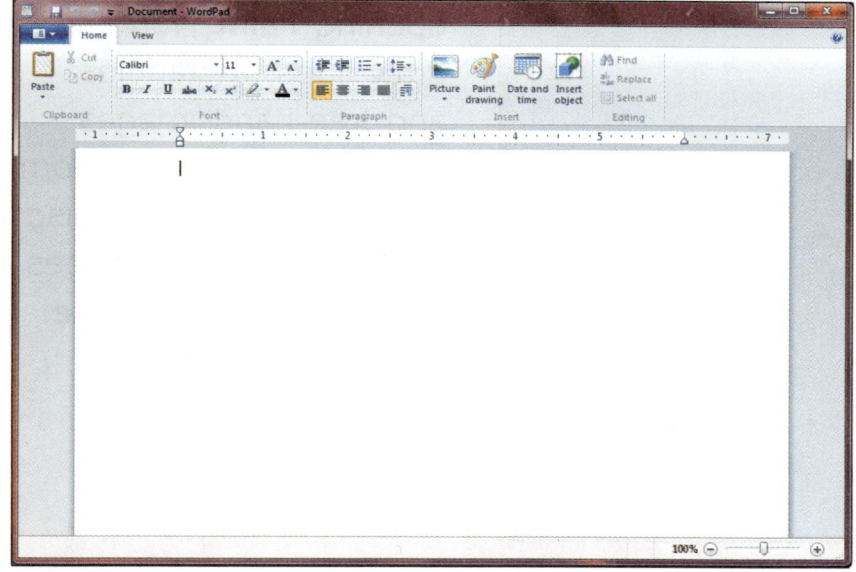

5. Type your document in the blank window. You can use tools and buttons in the text to format the text as you type it.

Drag and Drop Series

WORKING WITH MS PAINT

You can make use of the **Paint** tool to draw pictures. You can create logos for your business letters, create your own Clip Art and even paint pictures for your home or office. It is also useful for children as they can use this tool for preparing illustrations and drawing pictures for their classroom reports.

When **Paint** is opened, it displays a blank page on which you can start drawing. You select the line or shape you want to draw from the **Paint toolbox**, choose a color, and then drag the mouse pointer over the page to draw the line or shape. You can create pictures or illustrations by using various shapes and colors.

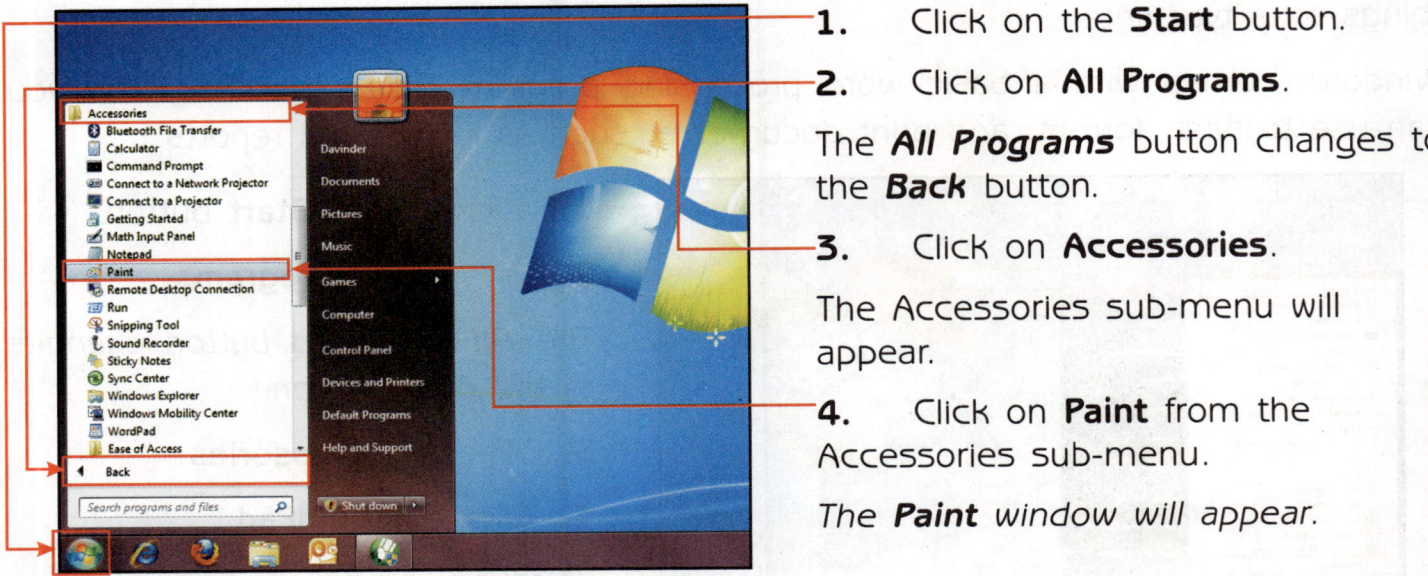

1. Click on the **Start** button.

2. Click on **All Programs**.

The **All Programs** button changes to the **Back** button.

3. Click on **Accessories**.

The Accessories sub-menu will appear.

4. Click on **Paint** from the Accessories sub-menu.

*The **Paint** window will appear.*

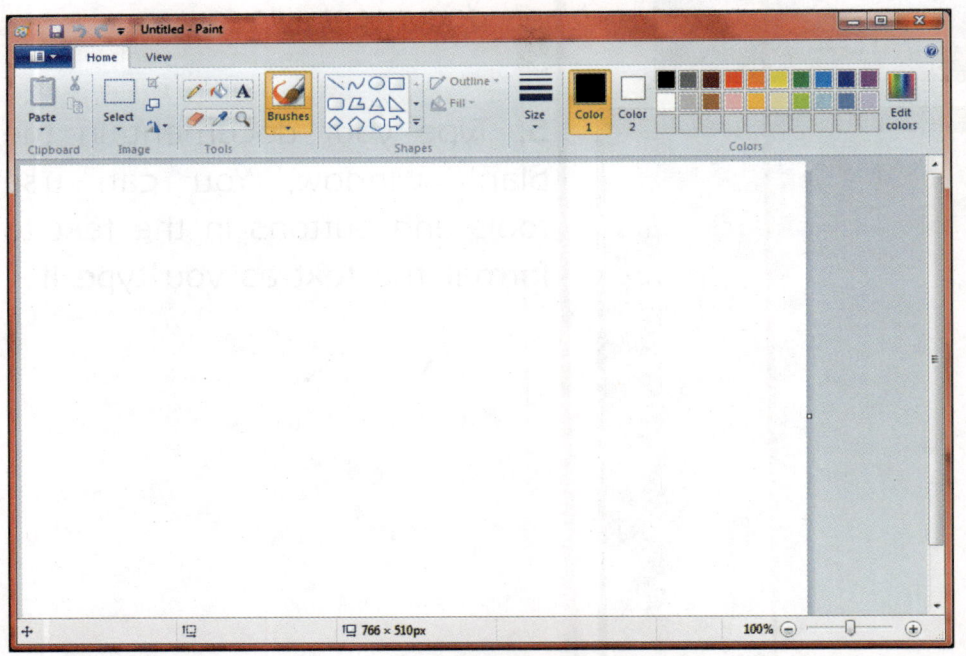

5. You can draw images and edit them after opening **Paint**. You can draw lines, rectangles and free-hand images using different tools from the toolbar. You can also fill color in those images using the **color palette**.

WORKING WITH CALCULATOR

For performing daily tasks, such as calculating the total due on a bill, we generally use a calculator. The **Windows Calculator** is very convenient to use. It is easy to use the **Window calculator** as it functions like any other simple calculator. You click on the number buttons to enter values and then you use the add, subtract, multiply or divide button to perform common mathematical calculations.

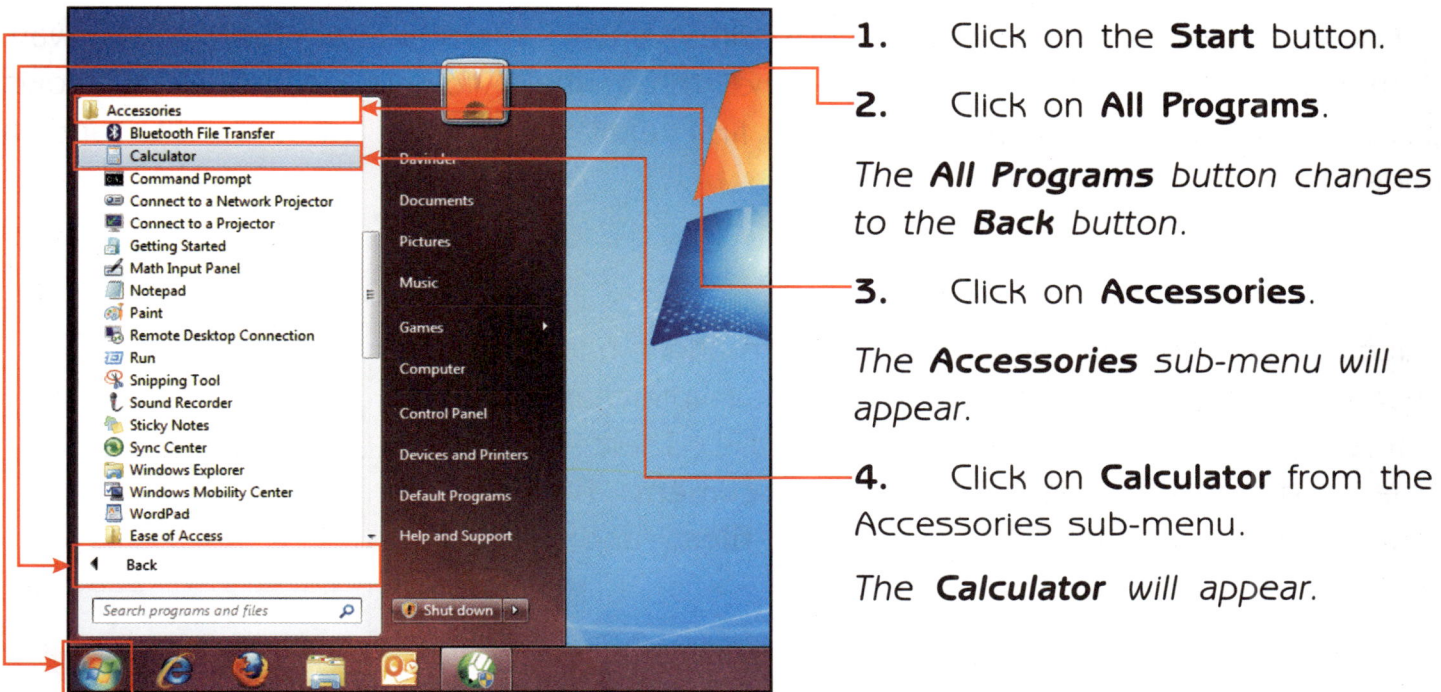

1. Click on the **Start** button.

2. Click on **All Programs**.

   *The **All Programs** button changes to the **Back** button.*

3. Click on **Accessories**.

   *The **Accessories** sub-menu will appear.*

4. Click on **Calculator** from the Accessories sub-menu.

   *The **Calculator** will appear.*

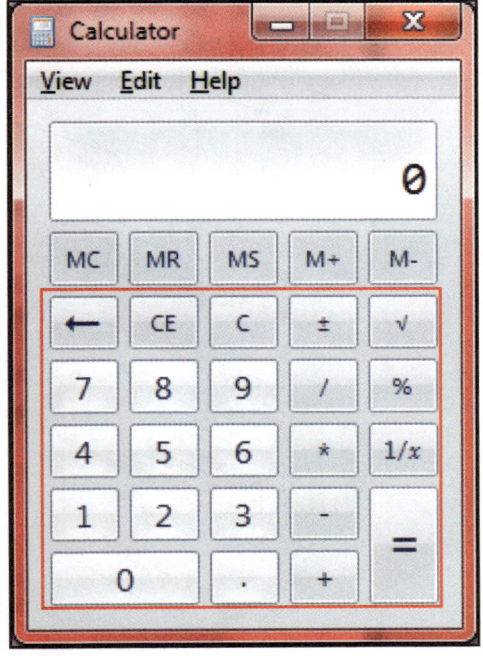

5. Click on the **Number** buttons to insert the values for a calculation, or use the number keys or numeric keypad in the keyboard.

4 Files and folders

FILES AND FOLDERS IN WINDOWS

Windows helps you to store your files and folders in a very easy way. **Computer**, **Picture** and **Music** are the three main folders in which Windows saves your files by default. Let me first explain to you, what a file and a folder is.

FILE : A collection of data or information has a name, called the **filename**. Almost all information stored in a computer must be in a file. There are many different types of files : **document files**, **text files**, **program files**, **directory files**, and so on.

FOLDER : Just like a file cabinet in school or at home, the computer also stores many files. There are thousands of files in your computer. Instead of dumping every file into your computer's hard drive, you can arrange them into folders. Most folders contain files. Some folders contain additional folders, which we call **subfolders**.

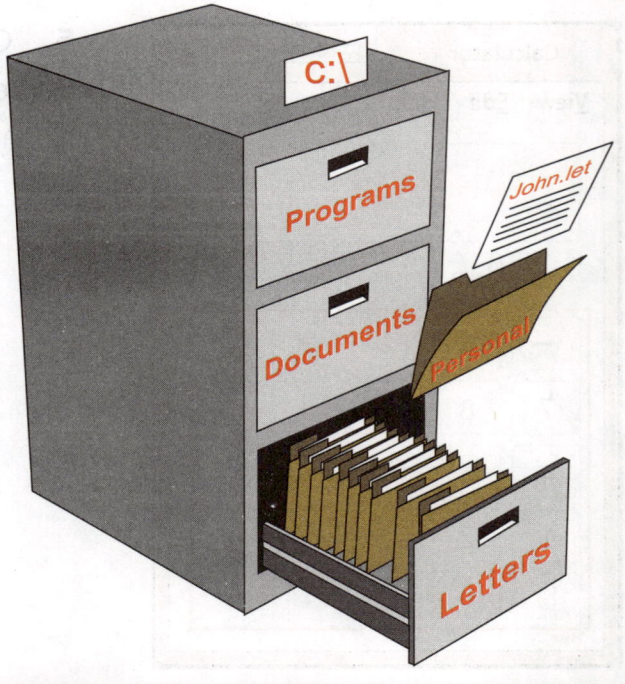

VIEWING YOUR FILES

You can view the files you create, as well as those that you download and copy to your computer, which get stored in your hard drive. If you want to open or work with those files, you first need to view them.

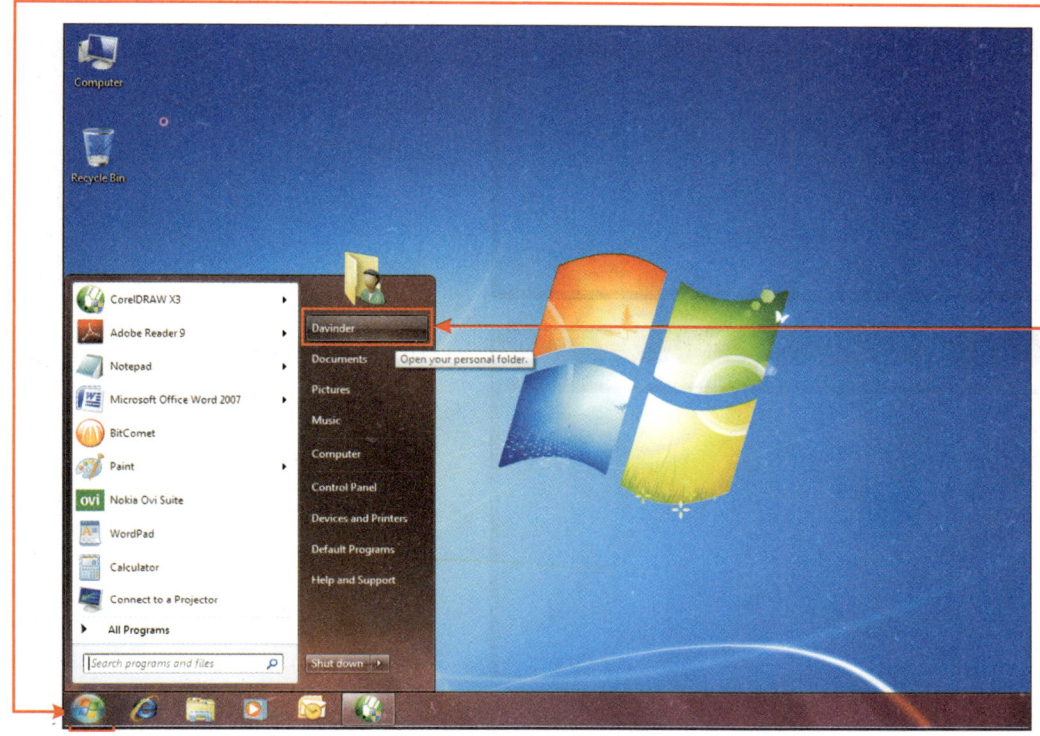

1. Click on the **Start** button to open the start menu.

2. Click on your user name.

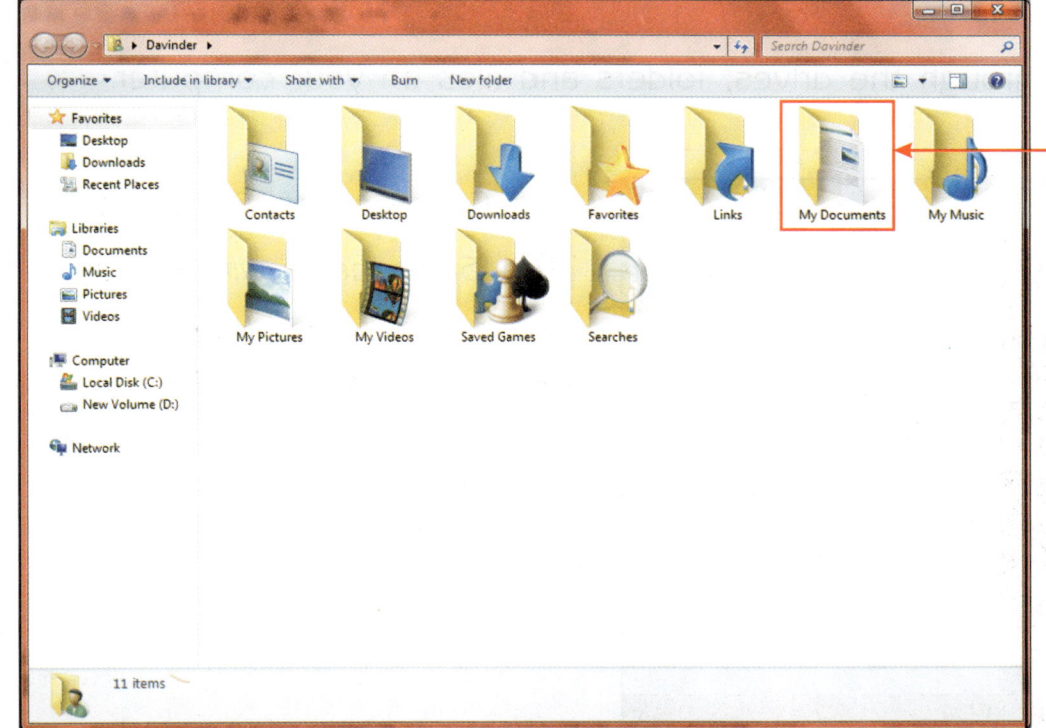

Windows 7 displays your user folder.

3. Double-click on the folder you want to view.

Drag and Drop Series

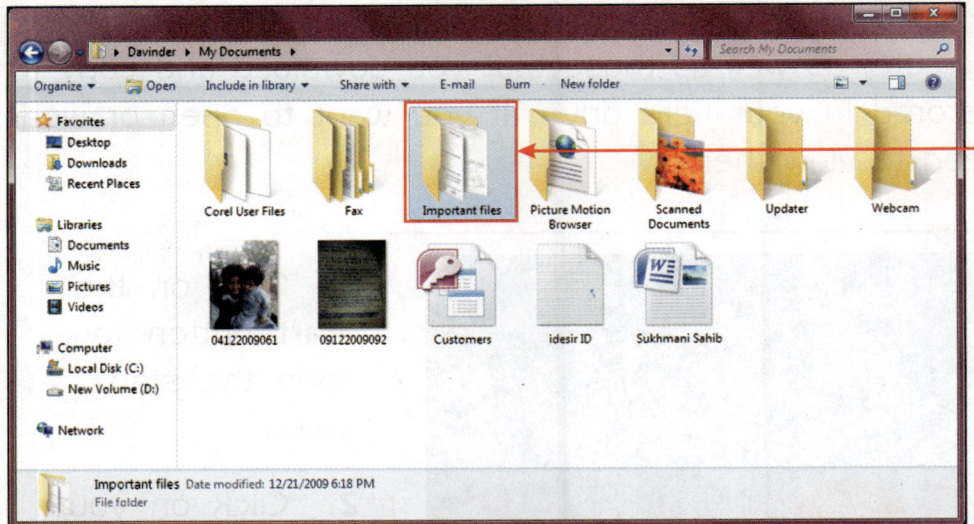

Windows 7 displays the contents of the folder, including subfolders.

4. If the files you want to view are stored in a subfolder, double-click the subfolder.

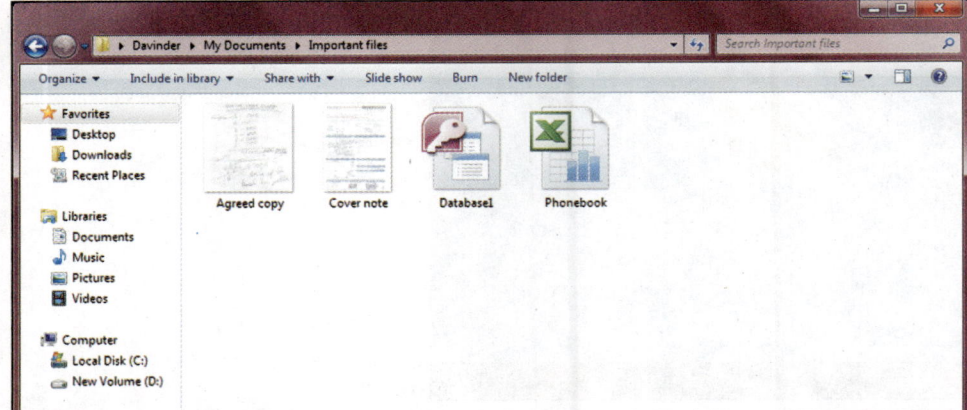

Windows 7 displays the contents of the subfolder.

MY COMPUTER

You can simply browse through the drives, folders and files on your computer.

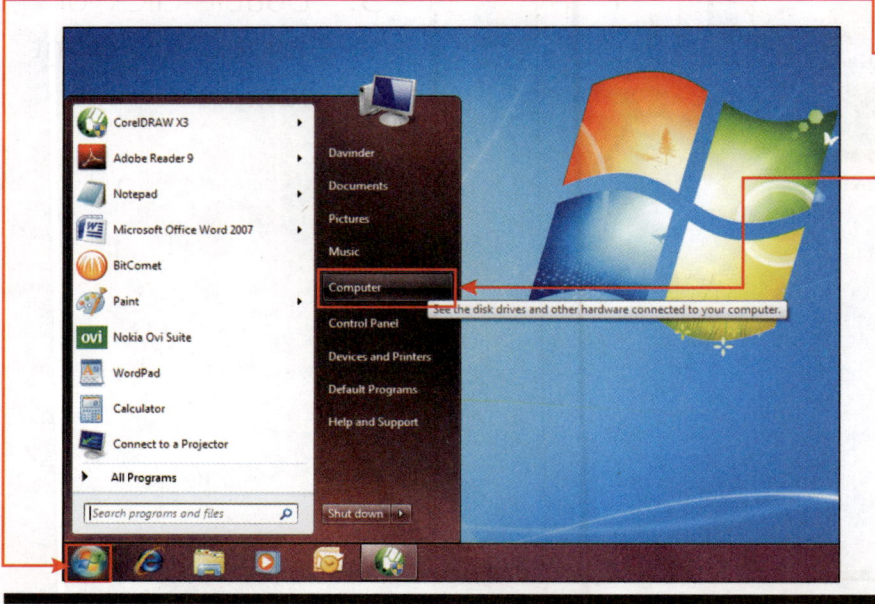

1. Click on the **Start** button.

The Start menu will appear.

2. Click on **Computer** to open **My Computer** for viewing the contents of your computer.

Windows 7

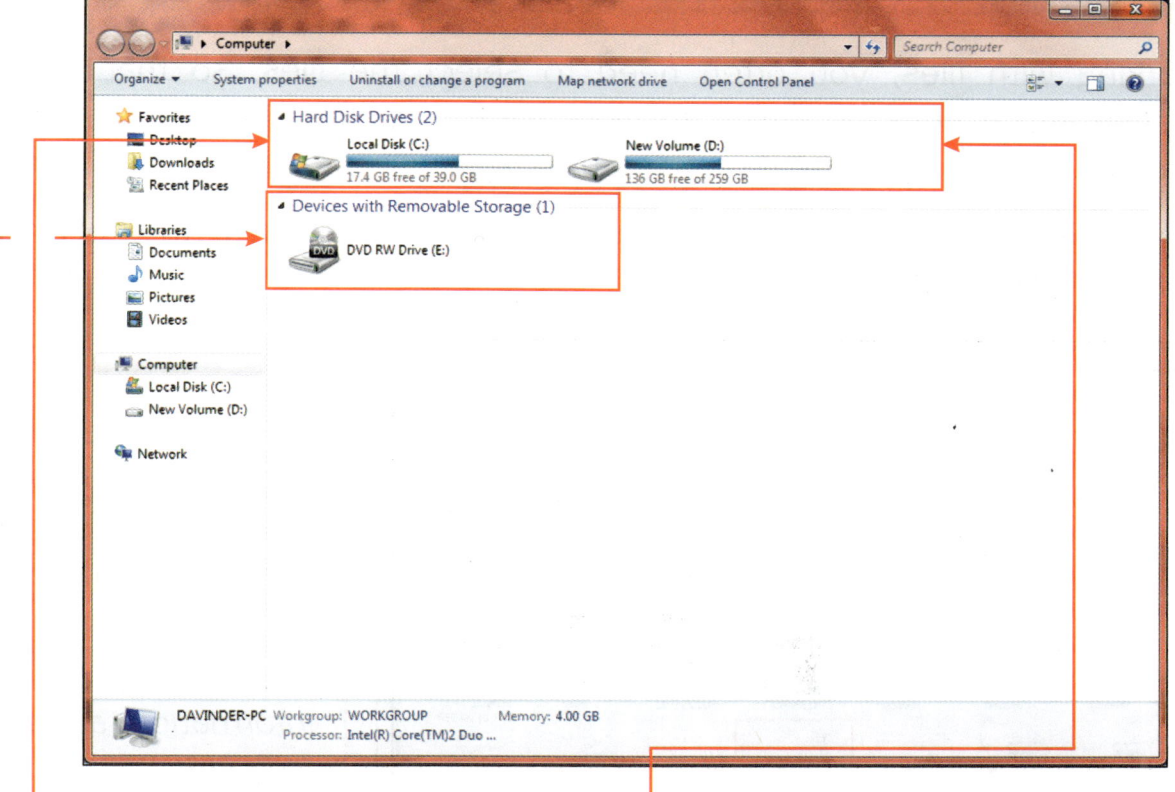

This area displays the hard drives available on your computer.

This area represents your floppy drive, CD-ROM drive and any other drives available on your computer.

3. Double-click on the item to display the contents of a drive or folder.

To view the contents of a floppy drive or CD-ROM drive, make sure that you insert the floppy disk or CD-ROM disc into the appropriate drive before continuing.

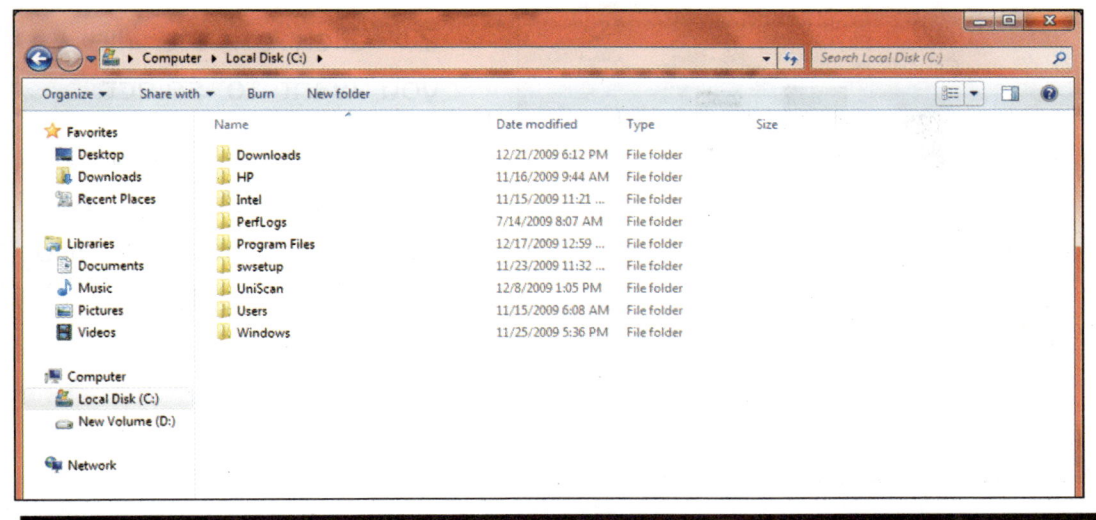

Windows 7 displays the contents of a drive or folder.

Drag and Drop Series

SELECTING FILES

Before working with files, you often need to select the files, so that Windows 7 knows exactly which ones you want to work with. Selected files appear highlighted on your screen.

Although you learn specifically about selecting files in this task, the technique for selecting folders is exactly the same.

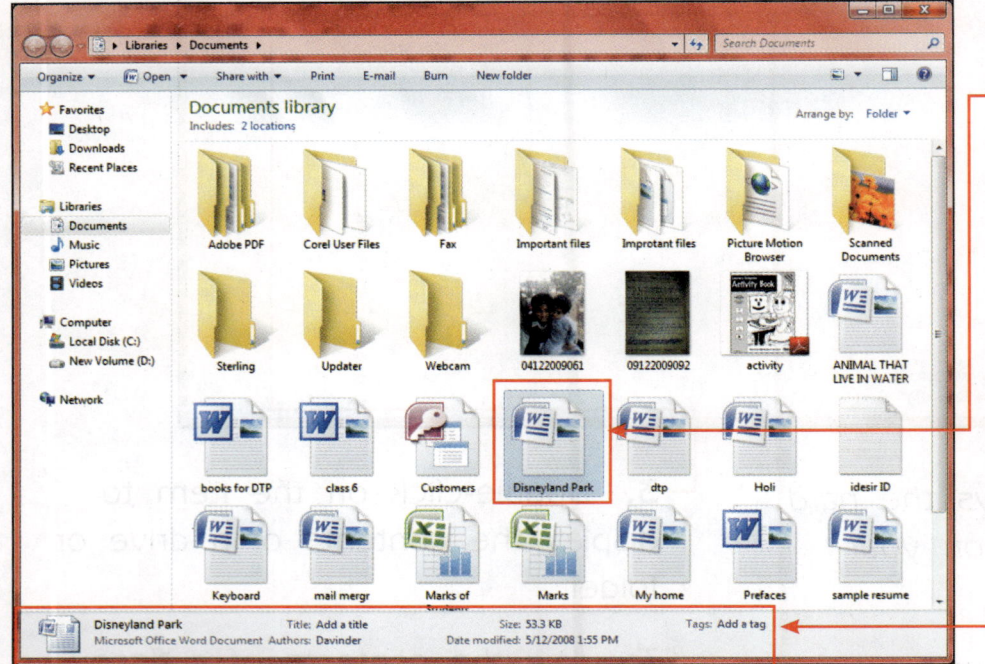

Selecting one file

1. Open the folder containing the files.

2. Click on the file you want to select.

The file is highlighted.

Information about the file appears in this area, including the file type, size, date and time when the file was last changed.

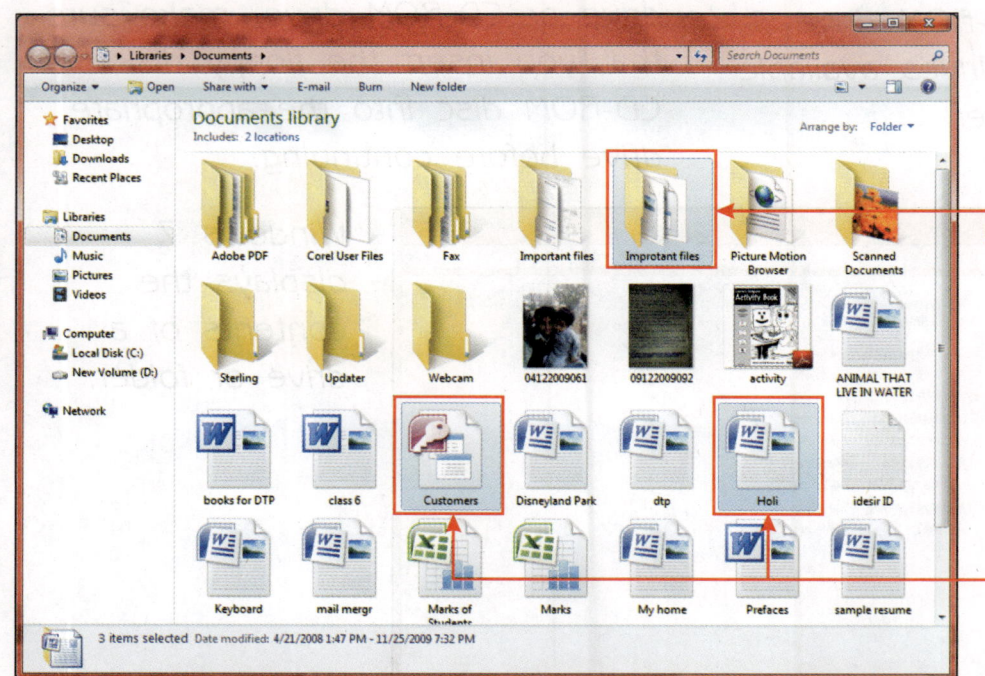

Selecting multiple files

1. Open the folder containing the files.

2. Click on the file you want to select.

3. Press and hold down the **Ctrl** key as you click each file you want to select.

Windows 7

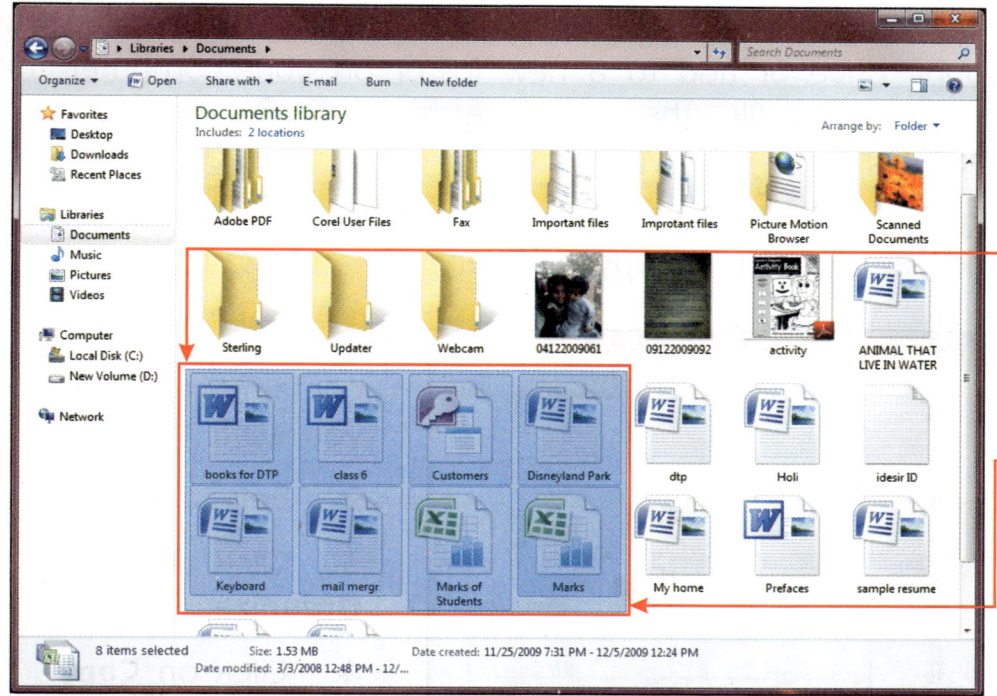

Selecting a group of files

1. Open the folder containing the files.

2. Position the mouse pointer slightly above and slightly to the left of the first file in the group.

3. Click and drag the mouse pointer down and to the right until all the files in the group are selected.

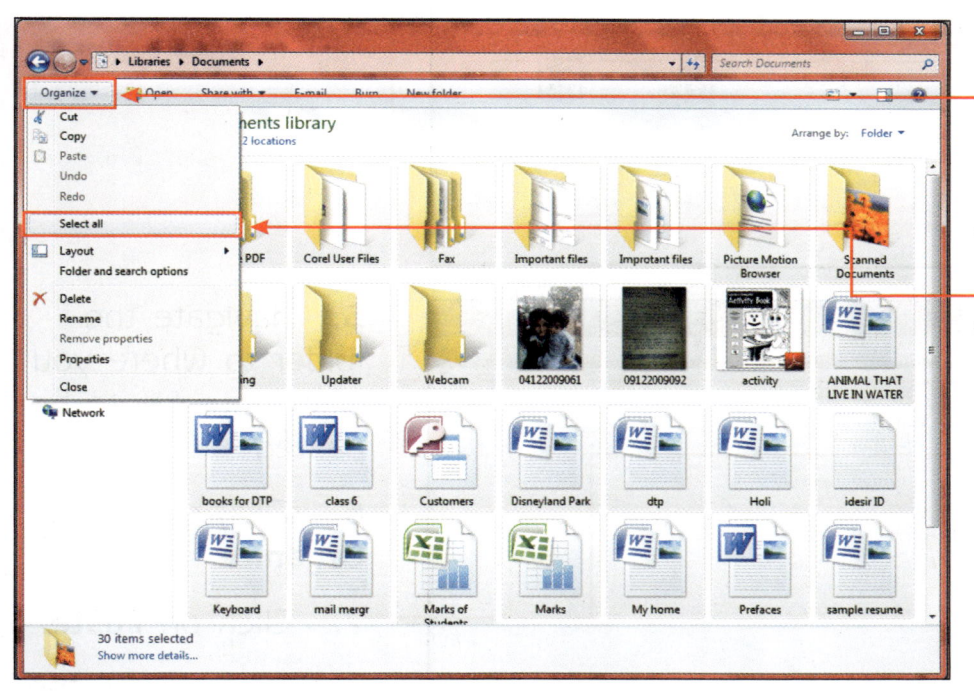

Selecting all files

1. Open the folder containing the files.

2. Click on **Organize**.

3. Click on **Select All**.

Windows selects all the files in the folder.

DESELECTING FILE

- To deselect a single file from a multiple-file selection, hold down **Ctrl Key** and click on the file you want to deselect.
- To deselect all files, click on an empty area within the folder.
- To reverse the selection—deselect the selected files and select the deselected files—press **Alt** key, click on **Edit** and then click on **Invert Selection**.

Drag and Drop Series

COPYING A FILE

You can copy a file on a floppy drive or add to a new folder on your computer to re-organize your files. When you copy a file, the file will remain in its original location and also appear in the new location.

In this task, we are copying a single file, but these steps also work if you select multiple files. You can use the same steps to copy a folder.

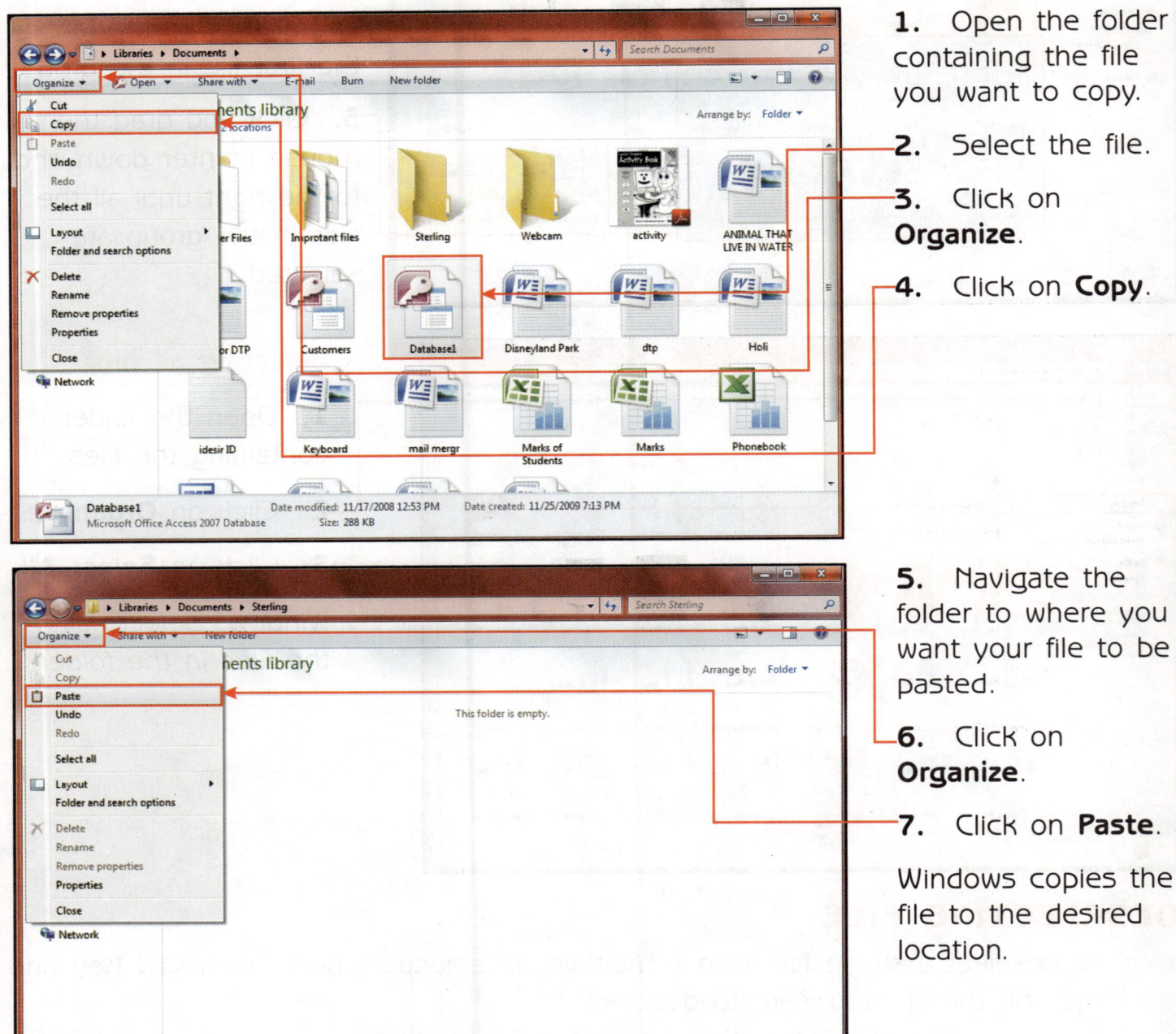

1. Open the folder containing the file you want to copy.
2. Select the file.
3. Click on **Organize**.
4. Click on **Copy**.
5. Navigate the folder to where you want your file to be pasted.
6. Click on **Organize**.
7. Click on **Paste**.

Windows copies the file to the desired location.

MOVING A FILE

You can move a file to a floppy drive or to a new location on your computer to re-organize your files. When you move a file, the file will disappear from its original location and appear in the new location.

In this task, we are moving a single file, but these steps also work if you select multiple files. You can also use these steps to move a folder.

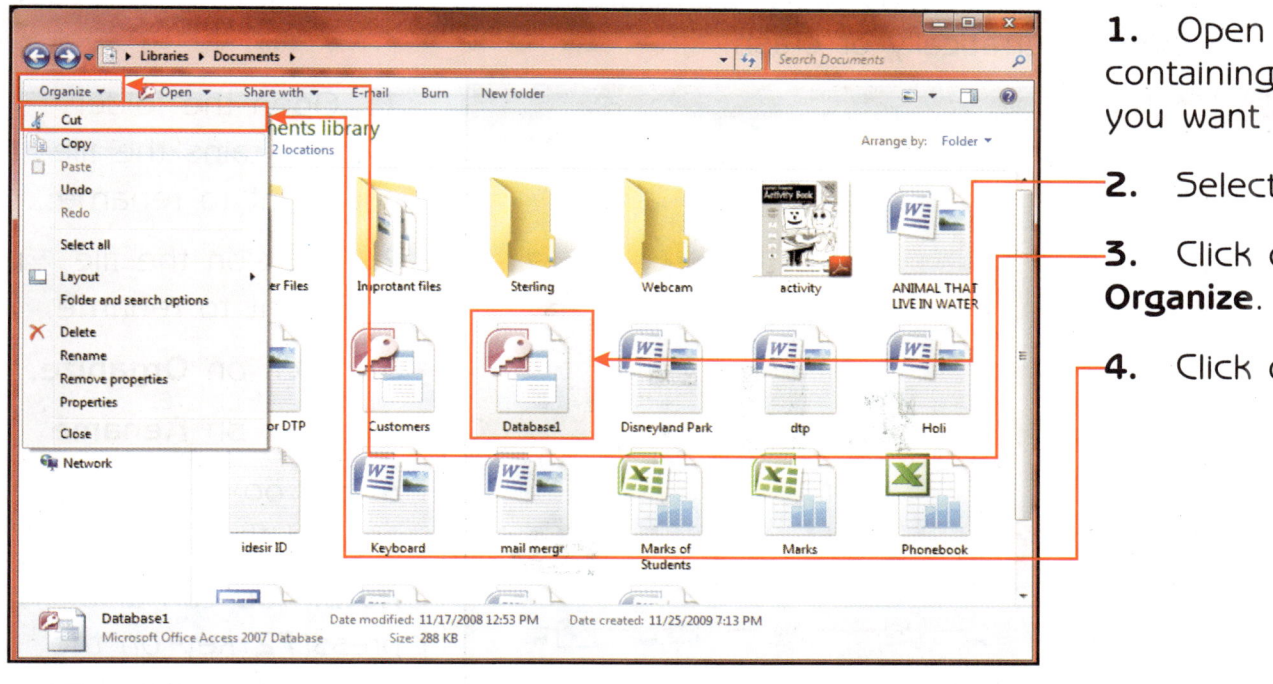

1. Open the folder containing the file you want to move.

2. Select the file.

3. Click on **Organize**.

4. Click on **Cut**.

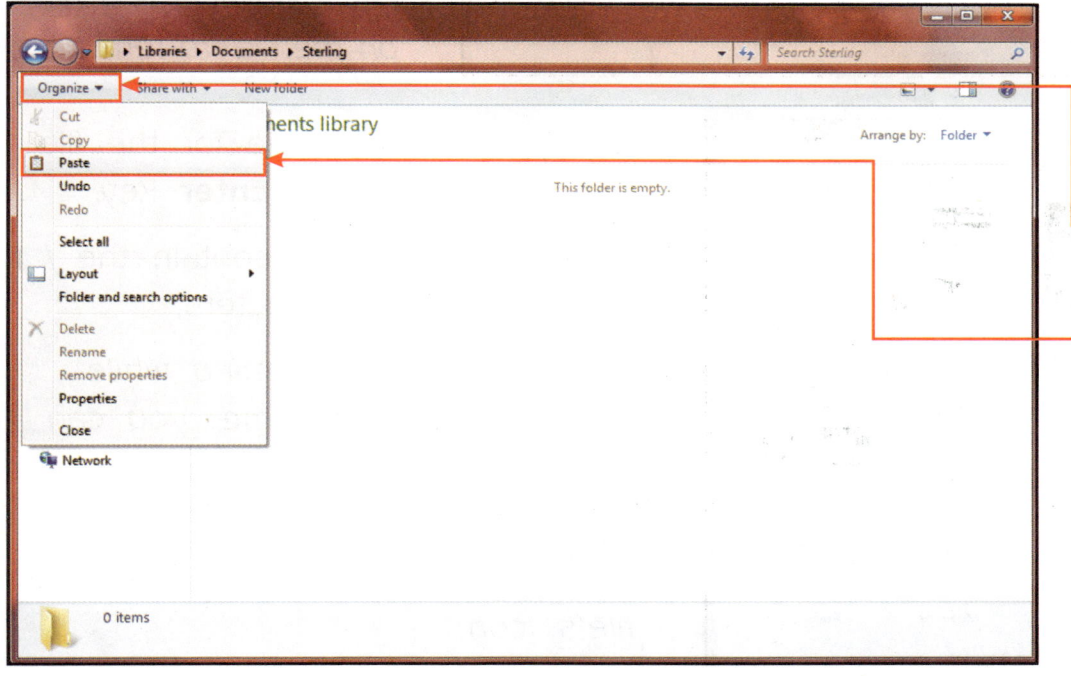

5. Navigate the folder where you want your file to be pasted.

6. Click on **Organize**.

7. Click on **Paste**.

Windows moves the file to the desired location.

Drag and Drop Series

RENAMING A FILE

You can rename a file for a better description of the contents of the file. Renaming a file can help you quickly locate the file in future. You can rename folders the same way you rename files.

Make sure that you only rename those documents that you have created yourself or that have been given to you by someone else. Do not rename any of the Windows 7 system files or any files associated with your programs, or your computer may behave erratically or crash.

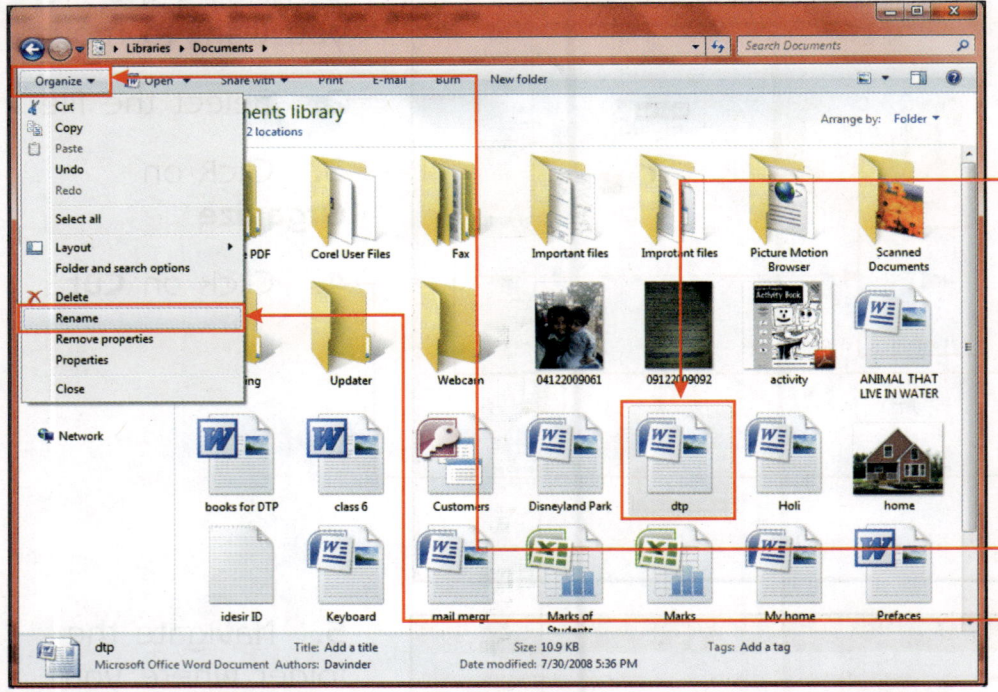

1. Open the folder that contains the file you want to rename.

2. Click on the file you want to rename.

3. Click on **Organize**.

4. Click on **Rename**.

A text box appears around the file name.

Note: *You can also press **F2** key on the keyboard after clicking on the file to rename it.*

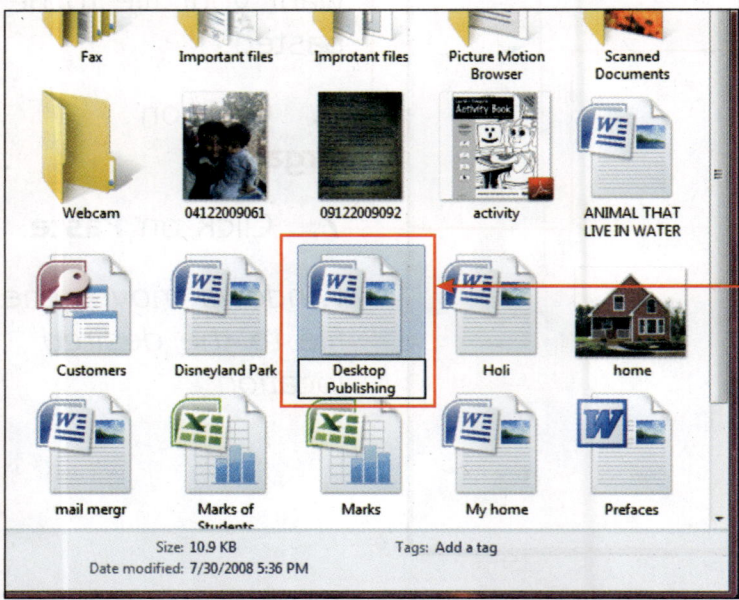

5. Type a new name for the file and then press the **Enter** key.

A file name cannot contain the / \ ? " < > or ! characters.

*If you change your mind while typing a new file name, you can press the **ESC** key to return to the original file name.*

The new name appears under the file's icon.

CREATE A NEW FILE

You can instantly create, name and store a new file in the location you want, without starting a program. Creating a new file without starting a program allows you to focus on the organisation of your files rather than the programs you need to accomplish your tasks.

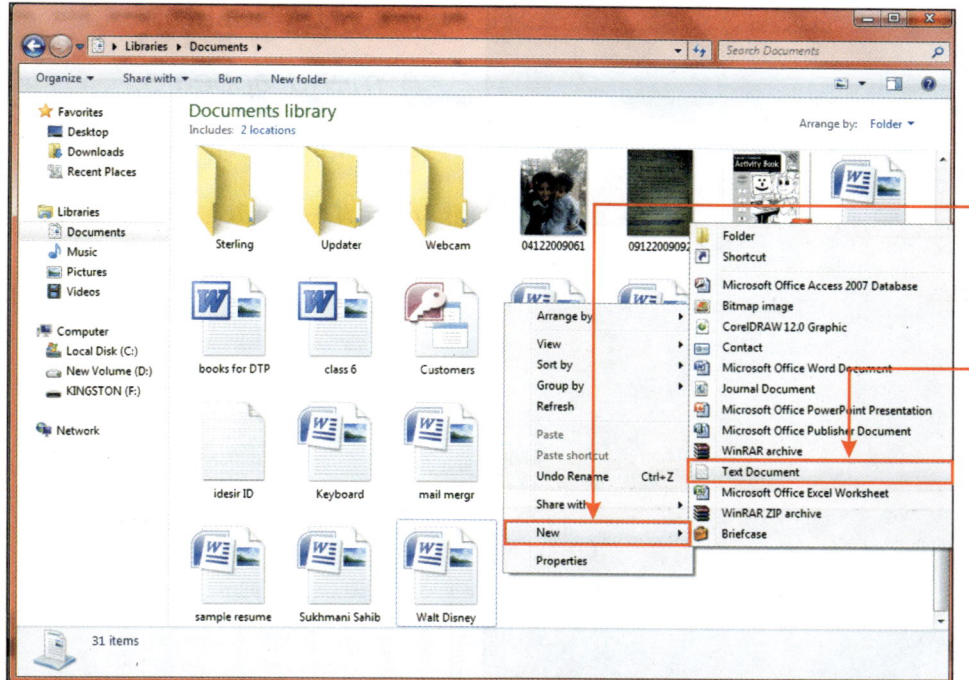

1. Open the folder in which you want to create the file.

2. Right-click on an empty section in the folder.

3. Click on **New**.

4. Click the **type of file** you want to create.

Note: If you click **Folder**, Windows 7 creates a **new subfolder**.

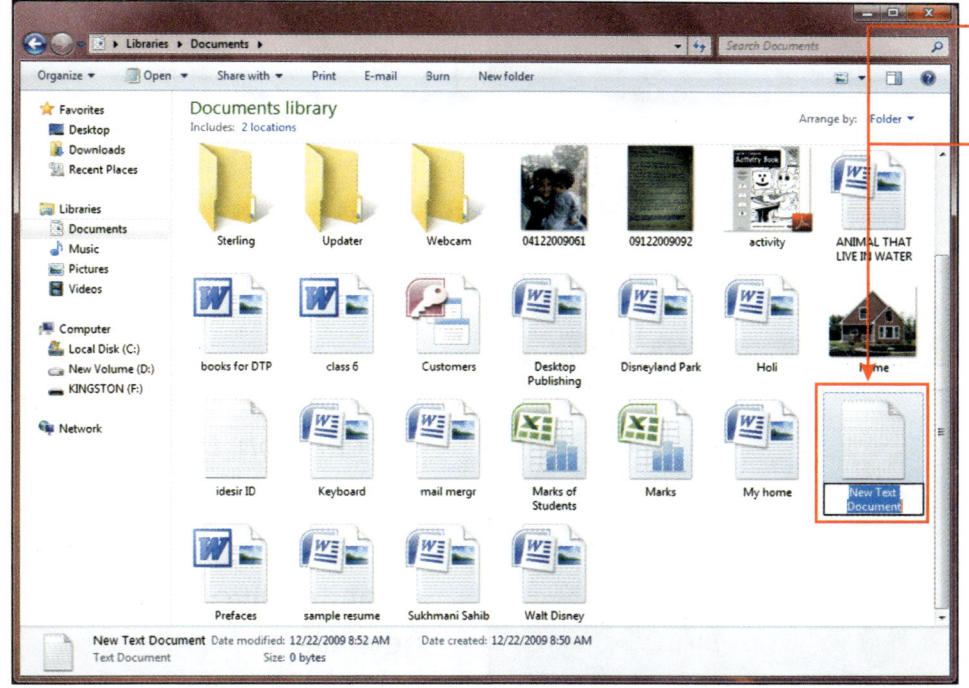

An icon of the new file appears in the folder.

5. Type the name you want to use for the new file and press the **Enter** key on the keyboard.

Drag and Drop Series

CREATING A NEW FOLDER ON DESKTOP

You can create a new folder to help you organize the files stored in your computer.

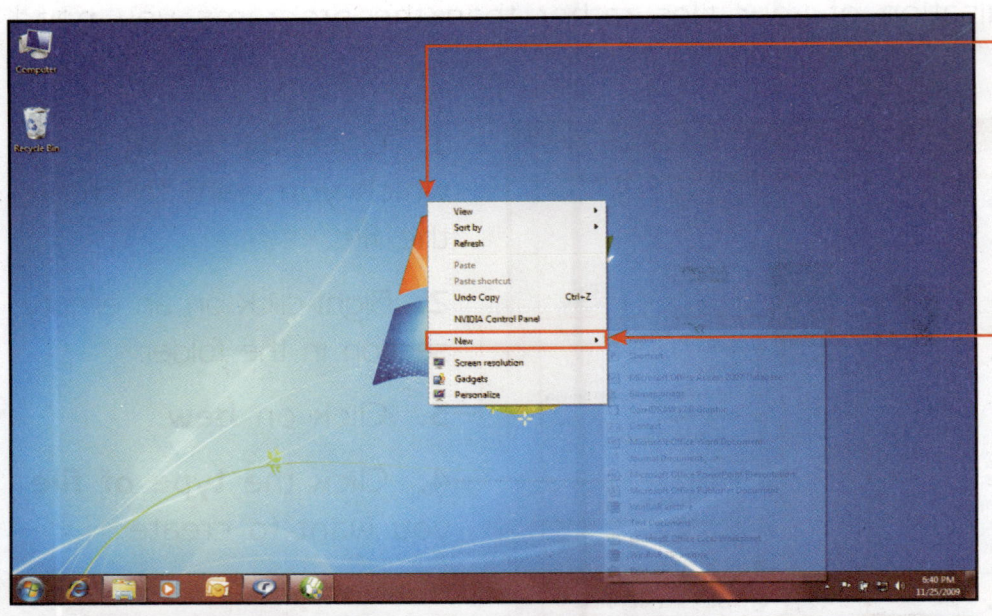

1. Right-click the mouse on a blank area on your desktop.

   A menu appears.

2. Click on **New**.

   A sub-menu will appear.

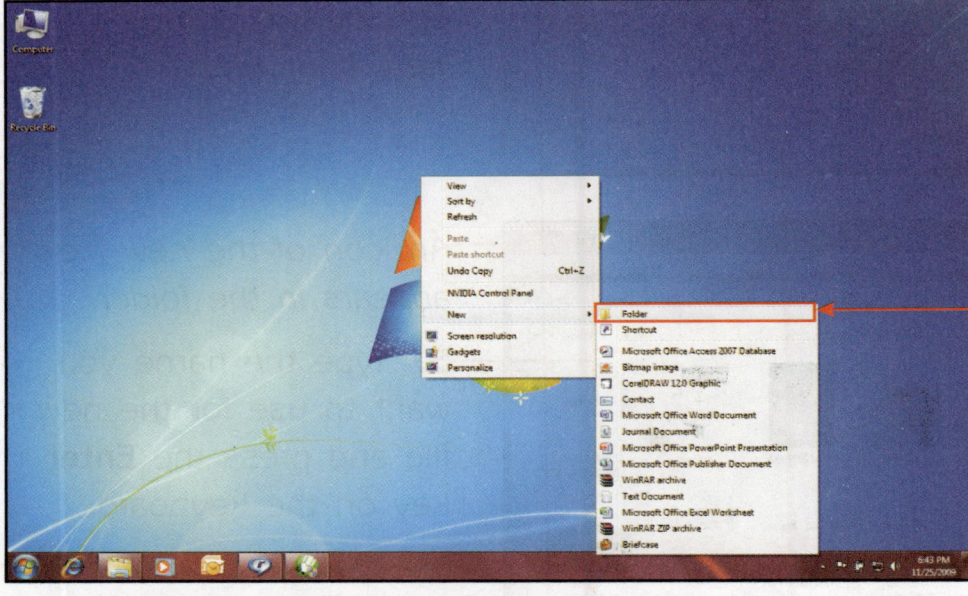

3. Click on **Folder**.

An icon for the new file appears on the desktop.

4. Type the name you want to give to the new file.

5. Press **Enter** key.

DELETING A FILE

You can delete a file that you no longer need. You should also make sure that you only delete those documents that you have created yourself or those that have been given to you by someone else.

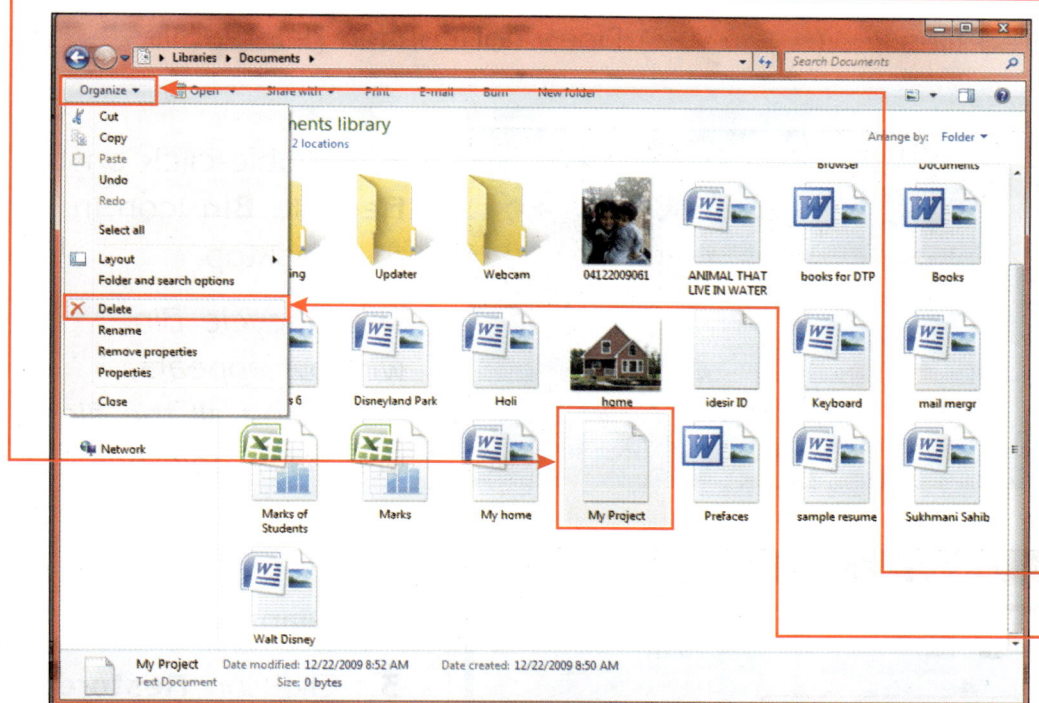

1. Open the folder that contains the file you want to delete.

2. Click on the **file** you want to delete.

Note: If you want io remove more than one file, select all the files you want to delete.

3. Click on **Organize**.

4. Click on **Delete**.

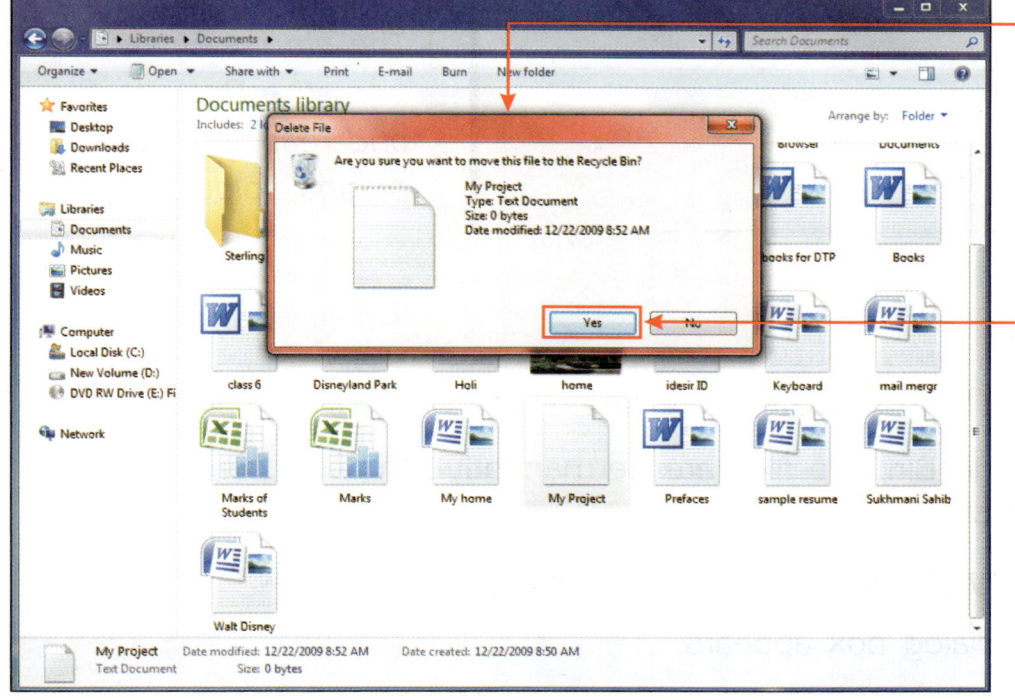

The **Delete File** dialog box appears.

5. Click on **Yes**.

The file disappears from the folder.

Windows 7

35

Drag and Drop Series

RESTORE A DELETED FILE

The Recycle Bin stores all the files you have deleted. You can easily restore any file in the Recycle Bin to its original location in your computer.

The appearance of the Recycle Bin indicates whether or not the bin contains deleted files.

() Contains deleted files.   ( ) Does not contain deleted files.

1. Double-click on the **Recycle Bin** icon in the desktop.

The Recycle Bin window appears, displaying all the files you have deleted.

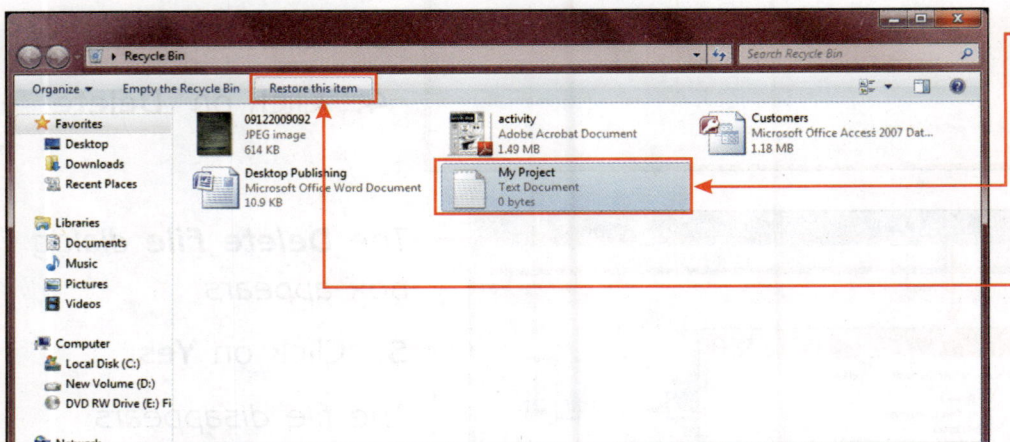

2. Click on the **file** you want to restore.

3. Click on **Restore this item**.

The file disappears from the Recycle Bin and reappears in its original folder.

EMPTY RECYCLE BIN

You can empty the Recycle Bin to create more free space on your computer.

When you empty the Recycle Bin, the files are permanently removed from the computer and cannot be restored.

1. Click on **Empty the Recycle Bin** button on the Recycle Bin window.

The **Delete Multiple Items** dialog box appears.

2. Click on **Yes** to permanently delete all the files in the Recycle Bin.

5   Playing a music CD

PLAYING A MUSIC CD

You can use your computer to play music CDs while you work. You need a computer with sound capabilities and a CD-ROM drive to play music CDs. The CD Player provides you with a control panel that looks and acts like the one you find on a real CD player. You simply click on the onscreen buttons to play, stop, pause and eject your disc.

1. Insert a music CD into your computer's CD or DVD drive.

   The **Now Playing window** appears and the CD begins playing.

   The album cover appears here on some commercial CDs, .

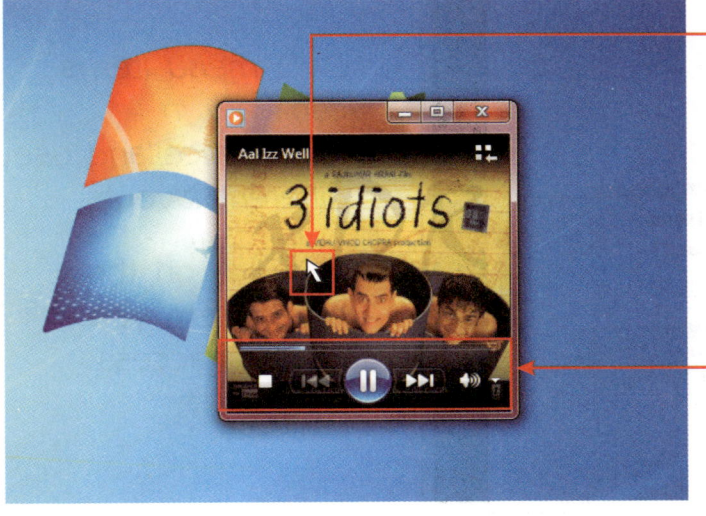

2. Move the mouse within the Now Playing window.

   The **playback controls** appears.

   You can use these controls to stop the CD and then select another song to play, or you can pause the song if you have to leave the computer.

Drag and Drop Series

PLAY A DVD

You can use Windows Media Player to play DVDs. Many times your DVD may begin playing as soon as you insert it. If it does not, you can follow the steps in this section to initiate playback.

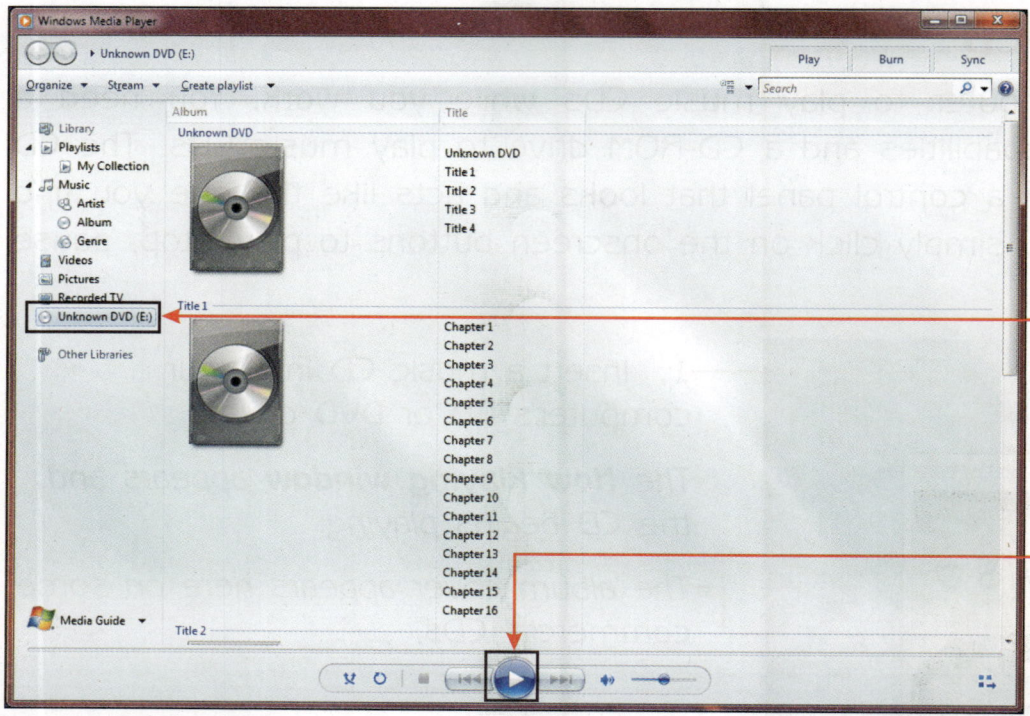

1. Insert a DVD into your computer's DVD drive.

2. Click on **DVD** in the Navigation pane in Windows Media Player.

3. Click on the **Play** button.

Windows Media Player plays the DVD and displays the in-built menu.

DVD menu items can vary in appearance and use different layouts.

4. Click on the menu item you want to access.

6 Optimizing performance

VIEWING THE HARD DISK SPACE

You can view the amount of used and free space on a disk. You should check the amount of free space on your computer's hard disk at least once a month. Your computer will operate most effectively when at least 20% of your total hard disk space is free.

1. Click on the **Start** button. The Start menu will appear.

2. Click on **Computer**.

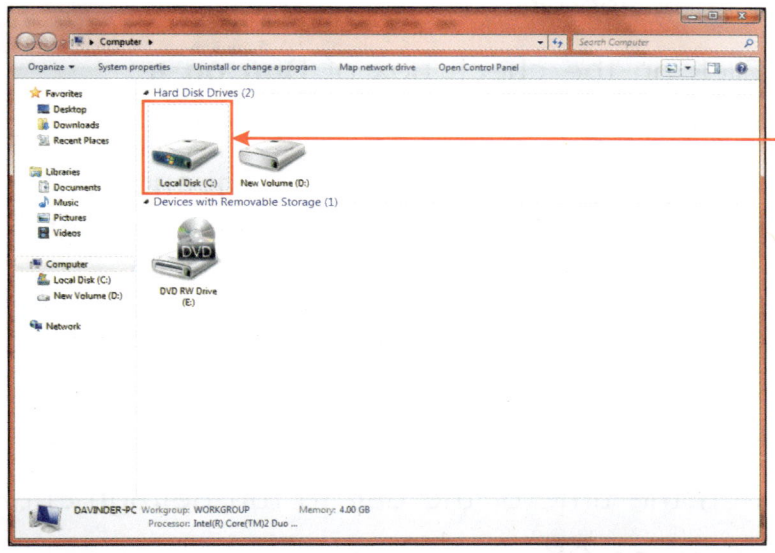

The **Computer** window will appear.

3. To view the amount of space on a disk, click on the disk of interest.

To view the amount of space on a floppy disk or CD-ROM disc, you must insert the disk into the appropriate drive before performing step 3.

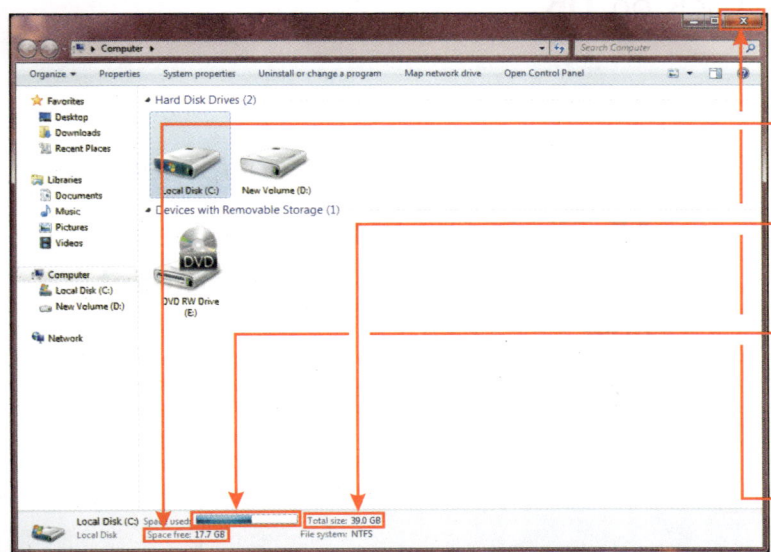

Information about the disk appears in the Details pane.

This value tells you the amount of free space on the drive.

This value tells you the total amount of space on the drive.

This bar shows the amount of free and used space and it turns red when disk space becomes low.

4. Click on the **Close** button to close the **Computer** window.

39

Drag and Drop Series

DEFRAGMENT YOUR HARD DISK

You can improve the performance of your computer by defragmenting your hard disk. You should defragment your hard disk at least once a month.

1. Click on **Start**.
2. Click on **Programs**.
3. Click on **Accessories**.
4. Click on **System Tools**.
5. Click on **Disk Defragmenter**.

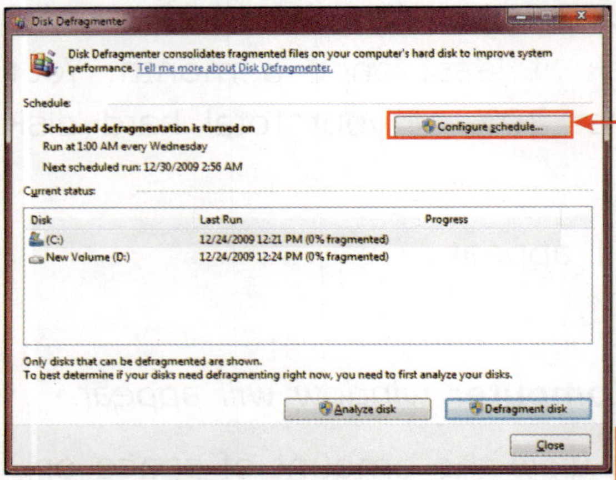

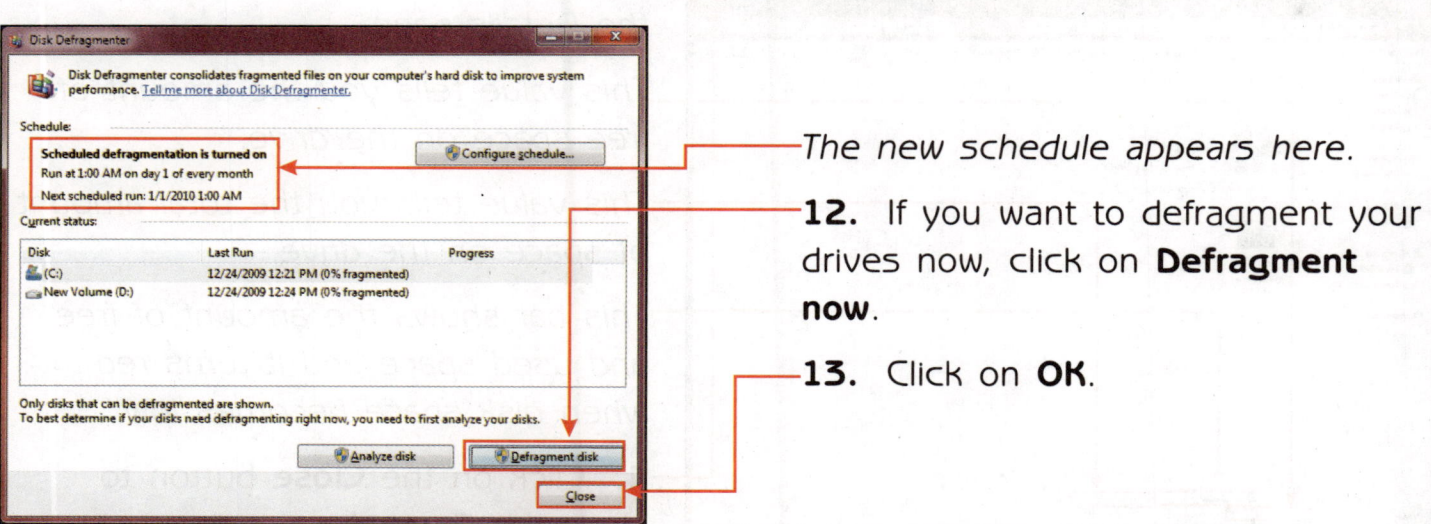

The Disk Defragmenter window appears.

6. Click on **Configure schedule**.

*The **Disk Defragmenter: Modify Schedule** dialog box appears.*

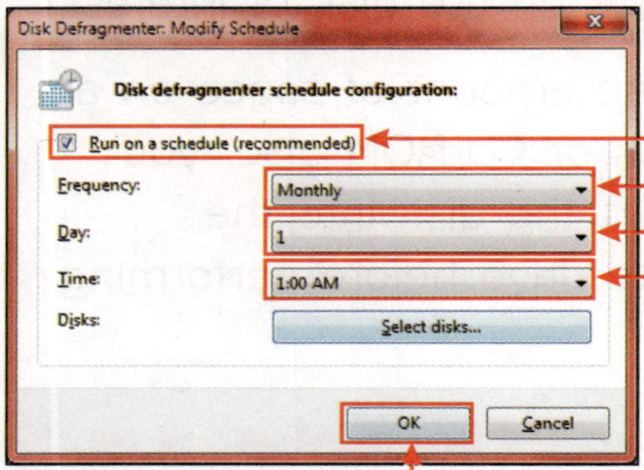

7. Click on the check box of **Run on a schedule (recommended)**.

8. Click on the down arrow of **Frequency** and then select the Frequency in which you want to defragment (Daily, Weekly, or Monthly).

9. Click on the down arrow of **Day** and then click on the day of the month.

10. Click on the down arrow of **Time** and then click on the time of the day to run defragment.

11. Click on **OK**.

The new schedule appears here.

12. If you want to defragment your drives now, click on **Defragment now**.

13. Click on **OK**.

40